PIONEERS IN PETTICOATS

By the Author

CHAMPIONS BY SETBACK
PIONEERS IN PETTICOATS

by DAVID K. BOYNICK

Pioneers in
Petticoats

THOMAS Y. CROWELL COMPANY - *New York*

To my mother, Rebecca,
and my wife's mother, Rose,
who also pioneered.

INTRODUCTION

FOR MOST of American history women have been, in the words of Susan B. Anthony, "not citizens but subjects."

It is only in the last half century that women have had the vote as a national right, achieved through the "Susan B. Anthony Amendment" to the Constitution.

For most of American history women were inferiors before the law, grouped with children and the mentally deficient. They were excluded from the professions and most occupations.

Custom rigidly controlled their conduct. The law said a husband could physically punish his wife with a stick and even prescribed its thickness.

Society found justification for this. Women *were* inferior to men, it believed. In the last century there even were some who argued that women were a subspecies of humanity.

This viewpoint has changed. Women have gained the opportunity for education, equality before the law, acceptance in professions and occupations, the dignity of freedom as individuals.

Heroic women, sometimes with men as allies, brought

the change about. They fought ignorance and prejudice. They went as pioneers into fields where no woman had ever been. They suffered denunciation, contempt, legal punishment, even physical attack.

Courage was their strength.

These are the stories of some of these fighters and pioneers in petticoats.

❧ Contents

Contents

Mary Lyon

FOR MORE than an hour the children had huddled before the window with a view of the path leading up the hill from the village. Aaron saw him first, a moving touch of black against the new-fallen snow, and he whispered excitedly, "It's Father—Father's coming!"

While the girls tiptoed to the bedside of their mother to tell her that Father Lyon was returning, Aaron wriggled into his coat, snatched his hat and ran out the door. Speeding downhill, he shouted, "Mother's had a baby—it's a girl! Mother's had a baby—it's a girl!"

Aaron Lyon the elder heard him when the boy was far away, and he too began to run. He fell in the snow, scrambled to his feet, and dashed on to the door of the little farmhouse. He drew breath into his lungs, brushed the snow from his clothing, and stepped inside, grinning broadly.

The midwife said, "It's a fat little girl, Aaron Lyon." He nodded, but his eyes were on his wife and the infant cradled in her arm. He knelt by the bed and kissed Jemima Lyon's pale forehead. "Praise be to Him," he said and closed his eyes in prayer.

Later he took down from its shelf the family Bible and

1

with a goose quill wrote in it the name which he and his wife had agreed would be given the child if it were a girl —Mary Lyon—and the date—February 28, 1797.

He gazed fondly at the sleeping Jemima Lyon and the infant, her silky hair almost white, with a reddish tinge, and then at his other children—Electa, Jemima, named for her mother, Lovina, and Aaron. To these other children he murmured, "It's a fine time to be born."

He echoed the feelings of his fellow Americans.

Every man was the equal of his fellows in the new Democracy. Opportunity was everywhere. Never did a land promise so much to effort.

Did a man want to farm? Here were rich acres for the cost of clearing the land. Was he a mechanic? Here were fast-growing industries pleading for hands—and the worker today often was an owner tomorrow. Did a man want to become a doctor, a lawyer, a skilled craftsman? All were possible. Will and work were the most important qualifications.

But all this opportunity and promise were closed to the new-born baby—she was a female. For her, and for all womankind, little had changed since the Pilgrims set foot on Plymouth Rock.

Mary Lyon came into a world in which women were regarded as the mental and physical inferiors of men—a subspecies of humanity, in fact. It was stated in law and acted out in custom.

"Man and wife are one, and he is the one," said the law. It meant among other things that a married woman could own no property, real or personal. At marriage all a woman owned passed into the control of her husband.

A woman could not make a contract, witness a legal document, sue or be sued, claim wages earned, or collect for damages to her person or character.

Even a woman's children were not hers but her husband's, the law said. He could give or will them away—even an unborn child.

In all America there was no woman doctor, no woman lawyer, no woman minister, no woman surveyor. All professions were closed to women and most occupations.

Woman's place, said society, was bounded by the fences and walls of her home; her duty was to comfort and console "her baron" while bearing and rearing a "quiverful" of children.

Thus it was in America. Thus it was throughout the world —and worse.

Now, fourteen years after the signing of the Articles ending the War of Independence, voices were sounded in demand for dignity and opportunity for women. They were few and feeble.

The stalwart champions of women were yet to emerge. One of the greatest was to be Mary Lyon. She was to found a college for women.

She grew to be a pretty child—sturdy of body, happy, and eager. The little rock-bound farm lying upon the highest ridge of the hill country overlooking the hamlet of Buckland in northwestern Massachusetts yielded only a frugal living to the toil of Aaron and Jemima Lyon. But Mary felt no want, not even when Rosina and then Freelove were born and there was a little less of everything. For the parents endowed the home with a richness of love and laughter and contentment.

For nearly five years she knew only happiness and then came her first sorrow. Her father died, not yet forty-five.

Uncomplaining, Jemima Lyon became father as well as mother and farmed the land with the aid of her thirteen-year-old son Aaron and a hired man.

It was evident that Mary was an inventive child. Once when she was a toddler her mother told her to brush the ashes from a bowl of potatoes which had been baked in the kitchen fireplace. The chore had to be completed in a half hour, Mrs. Lyon said. Mary worked at it with a brush made of a turkey wing. When only a few minutes of the half hour remained, Mary saw that she would not be finished in time. She pushed a chair close to the mantlepiece, stood up on the chair and reversed the hour glass.

"What are you doing, Mary?" Mrs. Lyon asked. The child answered, "I've found a way to make more time."

At five she began attending the little district school a mile away, later two miles. Sitting at a long table with the other girls and boys, the latter ranging in age up to sixteen, she received the rudimentary education of the day.

The education provided in the district school was of a poor and limited sort but a few years earlier even this was denied girls. She attended the school for two years and then for several years her schooling was irregular, a term here, a term there.

There were no permanent schools in the villages near her home, Ashfield, Buckland, and Conway. Schools were moved about or closed entirely when their teachers left.

The girl loved learning. For her the school hours were always fleeting. Having once opened the covers of a book she found it impossible to close them until she had read every sentence.

Mary had a mature way of telling about the things she had read and grownups enjoyed listening to her. At such times her large blue eyes sparkled with joy and the words tumbled from her lips in a rush. As she grew older she tried to space her words, practicing in private. She did learn to speak more deliberately but always when she was strongly moved the sentences poured forth in a breathless surge as in her childhood.

Mrs. Lyon remarried in 1810 and took to her new home in Ashfield the two younger girls. The three older ones were already wives. Aaron remained on the farm and Mary, thirteen now, elected to stay and keep house for him. For this he paid her one silver dollar a week. She saved this money for schooling and supplemented it with the earnings of spinning and weaving.

She was nineteen when she heard a piece of news which made her tingle with excitement. An academy offering instruction by a *college graduate* was being established in Ashfield.

She withdrew from its hiding place near the fireplace of her brother's farmhouse her store of money, hastened to sell two coverlets which she had made and enrolled in Sanderson Academy. Her brother Aaron soon married and bought a farm in New York.

The founder and principal of Sanderson Academy was the Rev. Alvan Sanderson, a Williams College graduate. Dying of tuberculosis, he had resigned his church to carry out a greater duty—aiding the boys and girls of the region to obtain an education.

The majority of the Sanderson Academy pupils came from more comfortable homes than Mary Lyon and at first she was an object of derision to them.

She came to school in a poorly fitting dress of blue linsey-woolsey with draw strings at waist and neck, in scuffed, too-large shoes. Her clothes were often rumpled and stained. Her manners were untutored and she walked with the long strides of a farm boy, her arms swinging loosely.

But the titters of her schoolmates soon subsided and they gaped at the feats of her mind. The principal had constantly to give her extra assignments, so quickly did she learn the class lessons.

One Friday afternoon Sanderson handed her a copy of Adam's *Latin Grammar*, congratulating himself on having found a task which would occupy her for weeks. The following Monday he called on her to recite, expecting a faltering review of a portion of the first chapter. After all, he hadn't aided her with a single explanation.

Her recitation covered the entire book, all the declensions, the conjugations, the rules of syntax—everything. The amazed pupils told their parents about the marathon recitation and the entire village talked about it.

But in her relations with others, Mary's friendliness, warming and pleasing, was more important than the power of her mind. She gained friendliness in return. Throughout her life it was never recorded that anyone who knew her disliked her.

Amanda White, the graceful, brown-haired daughter of Squire Thomas White of Ashfield, became her dearest friend. The Squire and Mrs. White came to love the happy farm girl and at the end of the first term of school adopted her in all but legal formality. Mary moved into the Whites' stately white house standing midway in the village street.

The Whites, descendants of generations of gentlefolk, schooled Mary in the social graces. "We did this because we loved her," said Mrs. White, "and because we were convinced that she was fitted for some important station in life."

Each evening Mary followed the portly Squire into his library and there, with great gentleness, he imitated her crude manners and then demonstrated the socially approved ones. Mrs. White instructed her in the choosing and care of her clothes, and in the care of her skin, her curly reddish hair, her work-coarsened hands.

With characteristic concentration Mary improved quickly but, oddly, remained all her life indifferent to her clothes. Amanda said, "I used never to let her out of my sight without inspecting her first. She was very likely to leave off some article of clothing or put one on wrong side out."

There was no play in Mary's life. Puritan New England frowned on anything so frivolous. But Mary and Amanda took walks together, read poetry, and attended church services and the occasional but deeply moving religious revivals. Sometimes Mary took part in a school play, which was acceptable because its theme always was a religious one. An old Sanderson Academy exercise program identifies her as "The Mother" in a play titled "Christianity in India."

Sparkling with health and animation, of a robust handsomeness, Mary liked boys. To one or two, said the villagers, she was strongly attracted. But she reasoned against marriage. Her intellect and interests, the villagers explained, were too greatly superior to those of the boys. And besides, she had already decided to enlist in the cause of woman's improvement. Marriage, she felt, would handicap her work.

Her particular field, she decided, would be teaching, which she liked. Already she had taught several terms in the district schools, receiving seventy-five cents a week and being "boarded around" with the parents of her pupils.

She became a full-time teacher at twenty-five, following a term of learning at Byfield Academy on Massachusetts' north shore in 1821. The school had recently been established by the Reverend Joseph Emerson, an ailing relative of the poet Ralph Waldo Emerson. Joseph Emerson did not agree with the prevailing view of women's intellectual frailty.

The next year—the year Mary Lyon entered fully into teaching—Emerson moved his school to nearby Saugus. In his dedication there he envisioned a day when higher institutions of learning for women would be regarded as essential as colleges for men, adding, "Where such an institution shall be erected, by whom it shall be founded, is yet for the hand of Providence to develop."

He had no way of knowing that the hand of Providence in a few years would beckon the sturdy Mary Lyon, whose mind, he had said, was the superior of any woman's he had ever known.

After Byfield Mary Lyon embraced teaching with a missionary's fervor, returning to Sanderson Academy as its first woman teacher. Immediately an old problem arose to plague her.

It was so difficult, she said, to hold the attention of her pupils and keep order. The winter months were the worst, for then the pupils huddled in front of the fireplace and whispering and mischief were encouraged by proximity.

Moreover, her pupils seemed charged with a demon of laughter and it needed but some inconsequential incident to release it. Struggling to master the situation, she was often betrayed by her own tendency to laugh. She would laugh as uncontrollably as any of her pupils.

"I have no natural dignity," she mourned.

But like countless other young teachers she learned the art of discipline; and she matured as a teacher.

The trustees of Sanderson Academy elected her preceptress. In her spare time she taught at nearby village schools. Because there were few qualified women teachers, she was much sought after by the handful of private schools in New England which offered education at a good level to girls. Later Mary Lyon served as assistant principal at the Adams Female Seminary in Londonderry, New Hampshire, and after that at Ipswich Female Seminary at Ipswich, Massachusetts.

Whenever possible she took courses to improve herself. Professor Amos Eaton of Amherst College gave her permission to attend his lectures on chemistry, experimental philosophy, and geology. Later, when she became well known, her male classmates remembered that she was a brilliant student—and that her shawl often trailed in the dust as she walked.

In teaching her girls she departed in many ways from the conventions of dour New England. She taught a philosophy of happiness. Tapping with a pencil on her forefinger for emphasis, she would say, "God wants you to be happy. He made you to be happy."

In a course she termed "Intellectual Philosophy," she even gave talks on sex education. In her time this was almost unheard of.

The years passed. The strong-framed girl with hair like reddish sand grew into a handsome woman, gracious and assured but natural and unaffected.

Her reputation as a teacher became widespread. Fathers came from far-off places bringing their daughters to the schools where she taught. Educators wrote asking advice or permission to come and observe her methods. School boards sought as teachers the girls who had studied with her.

She was an animated conversationalist, with a sparkling wit and a quickness of repartee. Once Catherine Beecher, a friend who was conducting a girls' school in Hartford, Connecticut, wrote her to arrange a meeting. Explaining that she was in frail health, Miss Beecher added, "I must be as calm as a clock, so PLEASE do not be too interesting."

Emerson had taught her that the purpose of education was "to fit one to do good." Mary Lyon defined this good in terms of educating girls. "Make them bigger than their fathers and mothers," she urged her teaching friends. She dreamed of a new race of women, strong of body, alert and mature of mind.

Her dream led her to undertake the bold venture which resulted in the creation of Mount Holyoke College and, by inspiration and example, the creation of hundreds of other women's colleges the world over.

She approached the undertaking with an initial reluctance; she was a teacher, not a founder of schools. But her code gave her no choice. "There is nothing in the universe that I fear," she used to say, "but that I shall not know all my duty or shall fail to do it."

How could she fail to know her duty when on every hand was the evidence of the poverty and chaos of women's education?

For girls both rich and fashionable there were several score finishing schools but these Mary Lyon accounted of little value. They taught mainly such things as deportment, a few French phrases for the drawing room, painting on china, fancy needlework, and dancing.

The majority of female seminaries, although they claimed

a more serious purpose, she rated only slightly higher. These were operated by men, and sometimes women, with little qualification for their work, without idealism. Their goal was making money.

There were only a few good schools for girls, established and conducted by a handful of men and women devoted to women's education—Sanderson, Emerson, Mrs. Emma Willard in Troy, New York, Catherine Beecher in Hartford, Zilpah Polly Grant at whose Ipswich Female Seminary Mary Lyon was now serving as assistant principal.

But in every case the principal was involved in a never-ceasing struggle to achieve basic physical needs for the school and to keep it alive. Often the struggle wore down the principal's health, as in the case of Miss Beecher.

She started her school in a Hartford store. She was happy over her progress when she was able to move the school into the basement of a church where "nearly one hundred young ladies had only one room, no globe or large maps and, most of the time, no blackboards and only two teachers."

Yet Catherine Beecher's school was valued as one of the best in the land for girls.

Although his health was poor, Emerson was compelled to travel about giving lectures for fees and take on a position as preacher in order to obtain funds for his school.

Ipswich Seminary was established by Polly Grant on the invitation of several men who owned an empty building which they wished to put to profitable use. But the principal had to purchase books and equipment from her own funds. Once when she wanted to buy equipment for the study of chemistry she was compelled to borrow the money from her assistant, Mary Lyon.

Mary Lyon knew the solution to the situation, as did Emerson and Miss Grant and Mrs. Willard and others. The solution was to be observed in the colleges for men— Harvard, Yale, Amherst, Williams, and the rest. It was endowment.

The men's colleges were endowed by private gifts. These paid for buildings, for libraries, for equipment, and assured the permanence of the colleges. They did not have to depend on tuition for their existence.

"Endowment!" exclaimed Mary Lyon in a discussion with Polly Grant, "It's the vital principle—and it's wholly missing from female education!"

So they decided—Mary Lyon and the dark, stately Miss Grant who also had studied with Emerson—to attempt to establish an endowed seminary for women.

They planned to begin modestly, utilizing Ipswich Seminary as a nucleus. In the winter of 1831 trustees were appointed and the two women set out to stimulate support for the school.

They met the same apathy and hostility which had balked previous efforts. The undertaking was shelved.

Later, in Polly Grant's absence due to ill health—which was to become a frequent occurrence—Mary Lyon turned the project in a new direction, drawing up plans for a "New England Female Seminary for Teachers."

This too failed to win support and in the spring of 1833 the board of trustees voted at a poorly attended meeting to disband.

Mary Lyon made an attempt to revive the project a few weeks later but little interest was aroused.

The labors of a year and a half had produced no tangible results. Exhausted from the multiple chores of teacher, acting principal, and organizer, she viewed the future with pessimism. "The indications of Providence appear to me plain," she said. "The only opportunity left is to disseminate knowledge which may operate on the next generation and come to fruition perhaps some twenty or fifty years from this time."

Others who had tried had come to the same conclusion. But Mary Lyon was of a different mind when she returned to Ipswich in September from a three-month tour of the Eastern Seaboard, New York State, Ohio, and Michigan. Renewed strength had brought with it a determination to try again—and also she had a new plan.

During the time that she was visiting her widowed sister Electa and her brother Aaron on the shore of Lake Erie, gazing at the military post in Detroit or observing the United States Mint in Philadelphia her mind was turning over the school project, analyzing, questioning.

Why had it failed? Why was so little support aroused? Why? Why? An endowed school would mean so much to women. If only there had been such a school when she was a girl sacrificing and working and borrowing for an education. It would have been so much easier—

Her thoughts ended in amazement. It wouldn't have been easier! True, she would have obtained a better education, and in one school—but it would have been just as expensive. She would still have had to struggle, work, and economize.

It had never occurred to her to plan to lower the tuition so the advantages of the school would be available to girls such as she had been. Without thinking, she had adopted the view of the time that higher education was primarily for the daughters of the well-to-do.

She felt an anger against herself. Naturally the public

had regarded the project with apathy. The great majority of people would have nothing to gain!

Eagerly she began developing a new plan. She would seek to create "a seminary which would be so moderate in expense as to be open to the daughters of farmers and artisans and to teachers who might be mainly dependent for their support on their own exertions."

During the year which followed she administered the affairs of Ipswich Seminary in Miss Grant's absence, taught her girls and gave over every spare hour to corresponding and meeting with prospective supporters. She also developed a new tactic.

The previous efforts, she felt, had been handicapped because women were announced as their promoters. And most men had a low regard of female intellect and competency outside the kitchen. Moreover they were angered when women spoke in public or identified themselves prominently with public issues.

She decided now to remain in the background of the new venture, subtly guiding it, while men of importance were announced as the prime movers.

On September 6, 1834, Mary Lyon, now thirty-seven, met with a group of leading men in her parlor at Ipswich Seminary. The majority had been enlisted by her good friend, the 65-year-old Rev. Theophilus Packard, a founder of Amherst College, whose daughter had been her pupil.

They included the Rev. Daniel Dana of Newburyport, the Rev. Edward Hitchcock, professor of chemistry and natural history at Amherst, the Rev. Joseph Felt of Hamilton, George W. Heard of Ipswich, General Asa Howland of Conway and David Choate of Essex.

The gentlemen, later to designate themselves a board of trustees, endorsed Mary Lyon's plan and voted to work for it. "But little did we imagine," said Professor Hitchcock some years afterwards, "that any of us should live to see the work accomplished."

They estimated that between $20,000 and $40,000 was needed to begin building. It was an unheard-of sum in connection with women's education. But Mary Lyon believed that it would be raised.

"Faith's business is to make things real," she said calmly.

She proposed a device used by expert fund raisers a century later—a fund of, say, $1,000 to finance the raising of the main fund. People considering making a gift to the school, she said, would be more likely to act if they were assured that none of their money would go to pay expenses of collecting funds.

She volunteered to raise the initial sum herself—and raise it from among women exclusively as a demonstration of the support of her sex.

She began in the Seminary where she was serving as acting principal. Teachers and pupils gave $269. She turned next to the ladies of Ipswich and nearby communities, going from home to home. One of her teachers, Miss Eunice Caldwell, told how she did it:

"She talked now with the lady of the house, now with the husband. She told the husbands in a good-natured but earnest way that she had come to get them to cut off one little corner of their estates and give it to their wives to invest in the form of a seminary for young ladies.

"She held out before them the object dear to her heart— the bringing of a liberal education within the means of the daughters of the common people. She put it to the lady whether, if she wanted a new shawl, a card table, or some other object of elegance she could not contrive the means to procure it.

"She spread out the whole subject, talking so fast that her hearers could hardly put in a word. . . . Ladies that in ordinary subscriptions to benevolent objects did well to put down their fifty cents gave her five or ten dollars of hard-earned money, collected by the slow gains of patient industry, and gave it of their own free will, yea, gave it as a privilege from which they would not have been willing to be debarred."

The ladies gave a total of $475. Mary Lyon turned next to her friends and former pupils, writing scores of letters asking for funds.

In less than two months she was able to announce to the trustees that the preliminary fund had been raised. Then she collapsed from fatigue and was unable to rise from bed for three days.

The campaign for the main fund was set in motion.

A young minister, Roswell Hawks, was engaged by the trustees for $600 a year to serve as financial agent. Mary Lyon withdrew from the public stage and went to live in the Amherst home of Professor Hitchcock and his family "to read, write, plan and do a thousand other things connected with the school."

She severed her connection with Ipswich. From now on she would have no income from earnings, only her savings of $2,000, and from this she intended to pay her own expenses in behalf of the planned school.

She began to write about the school, to speak to small groups in private homes. Roswell Hawks and volunteer solicitors—ministers and college professors who took an occasional week or two off from their work to aid the school —traveled about soliciting funds.

The first response was favorable. A number of people in New England approved of the project and gave money. The ministers associations of two Massachusetts counties adopted resolutions approving the project. This support was significant, for ministers had founded New England's colleges for men and provided most of the faculty.

From her position in the background Mary Lyon suggested to the trustees that progress would be aided if the school were "fitted to a local habitation and a name." The trustees approved of this step and in early January of 1835 settled on South Hadley, a pleasant town at the foot of Mount Holyoke in western Massachusetts.

The town's inhabitants pledged $8,000 for the school.

In April a name was chosen, Mount Holyoke, after the mountain—Mount Holyoke Seminary. "Seminary," a word which was then used to denote a school of any grade, was chosen instead of the term college because it was feared the latter might imply a rivalry with men.

Money came in from Hawks and the others, mostly in gifts of fifty cents, single dollars, two dollars, three dollars. The majority of donors were persons of modest means, but occasionally gifts of fifty and one hundred dollars were forwarded by the solicitors.

At first ignored by those hostile to the idea of an endowed college for women, the campaign began now to draw attacks and ridicule.

At a meeting a woman told Mary Lyon that she was aiming too high and charged her with an overwhelming ambition. Gently Mary Lyon replied, "True humility consists, not in self-depreciation, but in a just estimate of one's own powers or character."

Editors jibed at Mount Holyoke Seminary as a "whole-woman-making-school" and in a joke which circulated in the taverns a "disgusted farmer" was quoted as mourning, "They'll be educatin' the cows next."

William Seymour Tyler, a professor at Amherst College and a friend of Mary Lyon, summed up the attacks on Mount Holyoke in these words:

"It was called an innovation uncalled for, unheard of until now since the foundation of the world, and unthought of now except by a few strong-minded women and radical men, who would level all distinctions and overturn the foundations of the family, of society, of the church, and of the state.

"It would be the entering wedge to woman's preaching, practicing, lecturing, voting, ruling, buying and selling, doing everything that men do, and so overstocking all the trades and professions. At the same time it was insisted that such occupations as mathematics and philosophy were not suited to the tastes or capacities of women; they didn't want them and wouldn't undertake them; and if they did, they would ruin their health, impair their gentleness, delicacy, modesty, and refinement, unsex them, and unfit them for their proper sphere."

In February of 1836 Governor Edward Everett signed a charter of incorporation authorizing the trustees of Mount Holyoke Seminary "to hold real and personal estate not exceeding in value one hundred thousand dollars."

One writer said the news was received by Mary Lyon as a sign "that the kingdom of letters had been divided."

But now, at the peak of their hopes, a pessimistic note crept into the reports from Hawks and the other solicitors. People were complaining of hard times; money was tight.

Abruptly the situation worsened in a prelude to the economic panic of 1837. The flow of gifts dwindled to a trickle. Wrote one of the volunteer solicitors, "I find it impossible to obtain even a promise of a gift when the times improve."

Hawks traveled for three months, visiting merchants, clergymen, farmers, and artisans and wrote, "I have only an empty purse to show for my travel—I have failed to obtain a cent."

The more timid among the school's supporters advised that the project be suspended until the economy started on an upswing. The trustees looked to Mary Lyon for a decision.

She went at this time to visit her mother in Ashfield. Several days after her arrival a neighbor asked her mother what she thought Mary would do. Her mother answered, "Mary will not give up. She just walks the floor and says over and over again, when all is so dark, 'Commit thy way unto the Lord, trust also in Him, and He shall bring it to pass. Women must be educated—they *must!*' "

Soon she showed her determination in a daring action which left her friends aghast and the enemies of the school speechless with rage. She took the field herself as a solicitor for funds.

By stagecoach, carriage, or sleigh she traveled the highways and byways to visit prospective patrons, tell the story of Mount Holyoke, and appeal for funds.

Many men refused to admit her to their homes because

she was doing so radical and shocking a thing. Often women also refused to talk with her. The look of cheerful determination never left her face. She would bid the householder a polite good-by and go on to the next home.

Most often though she was given a hearing and many men who thought at first that her cause was fantastic and revolutionary ended, to their surprise, by making a contribution or a pledge.

She got results.

A friend, marveling at her effectiveness where the male solicitors had failed, said, "She held people in a sort of enchanted circle . . . by invisible attractions which it was hard to resist and from which very few wished to be released."

On an overnight visit to Middlefield, not far from South Hadley, she was received by a farmer who told her at the outset, "But your school doesn't mean anything to me. I have five sons—no daughters."

"I'd like to tell you about Mount Holyoke just the same," she said. The farmer agreed to listen and when she left two hours later it was with a cash gift of $100. Before quitting Middlefield she obtained $200 more.

Often people made donations at great sacrifice. One such donation is illustrated by several smoke-blackened dollars displayed at Mount Holyoke College.

In the village of Conway Mary Lyon called on two spinsters, Anne and Lucy Maynard, who were so moved by her appeal that they pledged $200 from their small income. A short time later the women's home was burned to the ground by a fire left to cook their dinner.

The next day, poking among the ashes, the two sorrowing

women recovered several silver dollars which they had set aside as the beginning of their fund for Mount Holyoke.

Declining to cancel their pledge, Anne and Lucy Maynard obtained work at sewing and weaving and earned the money for their gift and when finally they sent it in the smoke-darkened coins were included in the $200.

But Mary Lyon would not allow the coins, symbolic of great sacrifice, to be spent. She kept them and substituted an equal amount from her own funds.

Later she told her girls at Mount Holyoke of another instance of sacrifice. "At a time when everything appeared dark with Egyptian darkness," she said, "I went to visit Mr. Joseph Avery, who became one of our trustees, and his wife.

"Mr. Avery, a farmer, had already given to the school and I was reluctant to ask him to give again. However, I did acquaint him with our plight.

"When I had finished, Mr. Avery looked across to his wife and said, 'I had set aside a sum of money for shingling the house this year.' And Mrs. Avery said, 'I can set the milk pans under the leaky places for another year.'

"Thus these good people with three sons and three daughters gave another gift to the school."

Often though she traveled for days, clutching a green velvet bag in which she kept the gifts, without obtaining a penny. On three occasions her visits were rewarded with gifts of six cents.

On only one occasion did she show anger. This resulted from a fruitless visit, in the company of Squire and Mrs. White, to the home of a wealthy family in Ashfield. On her return to the Whites' home she sank into a chair, struggling to retain her composure.

"They live in a costly home," she whispered, "it's full of costly things, they wear costly clothes"—closing her eyes as though in pain—"but, oh, they're such little bits of folks."

The times grew worse. She worked all the harder, traveled ceaselessly.

"It's almost impossible for me to predict my own movements," she wrote Polly Grant from South Hadley. "I spent last Wednesday night at Belchertown, Thursday night at Barre, Friday night at Amherst, and returned here yesterday. I leave tomorrow on an excursion around the hills for the sake of conversation with some individuals about our enterprise."

Thus was Mount Holyoke won, in visits to homes beyond count, in appeals to groups of people in village churches, district schoolhouses and private parlors.

She spoke simply to groups but every man, every woman felt the singleness of her appeal. "Mount Holyoke," she would say, "will light a torch which will gleam throughout the world, and it depends upon you and upon me." Concluding, she would say, "Don't think any gift too small. I want the twenties and the fifties, but the dollars and half dollars, with prayer, go a great way. We are to have prayer in the new school, so let it be gifts with prayer."

Occasionally she was jeered at by strangers or criticized by friends for her "unladylike behavior." Finally she burst out to a friend who had voiced such a criticism, "My heart is sick, my soul is pained with this empty gentility, this genteel nothingness. I am doing a great work. I cannot come down."

Her courage, her work, and her determination inspired

the trustees and the solicitors with an awed belief she couldn't fail.

Early in the fund campaign the trustees had voted to begin construction when cash on hand and pledges totaled $25,000. In late winter of 1837 Mary Lyon added up the gifts and pledges entered in her account book. They came from 1,800 persons in ninety-one communities—and they totaled some $27,000.

The five-story building began to go up and Mary Lyon, watching the workmen, exclaimed, "The stones and brick and mortar speak a language which vibrates through my very soul." November 8 was announced as opening day.

The trustees appointed her as principal and Eunice Caldwell, who had been one of her teachers at Ipswich, as assistant principal, both to receive $200 a year and board.

There was no money for furnishing the forty chambers and for this the principal once again turned to women. Women of various towns got together at her suggestion to equip a chamber or raise the $50 to $60 needed to buy furnishings for it.

She prompted other women to contribute crockery, kitchen utensils, to collect feathers for ticks and pillows, to sew bedding.

When by midsummer the supply of furnishings appeared inadequate she obtained a personal loan of $500 to buy more and appealed to the parents of girls accepted for admission to the school.

There was no lack of applicants. Many more than could be accommodated applied. At the principal's request a number of those who had been accepted came to Mount Holyoke two weeks early to help with household duties.

Women of the village came also and organized working bees while their sons and husbands unloaded furniture from vans and set things in their proper place.

Out of this activity developed the romance, and in time the marriage, of one of the Mount Holyoke girls, Nancy Everett of Wrentham, Massachusetts, and John Dwight, a young man of the village.

They met while he was cording her bedstead.

November 8, 1837.

The dawn sun threw its rays on Mount Holyoke to the north and Mount Tom across the Connecticut River to the west.

It brought a stirring of life in the village of South Hadley. In the center of the village men and women were already at work in an unadorned building, ninety-four feet by fifty, the home of Mount Holyoke Seminary.

The school was not yet finished. One trustee was helping lay out the front threshold. Others were engaged with paint brush, hammer, and saw. Their wives were preparing food in the kitchen, hanging curtains, and making beds.

Girls accepted for the first year class of seventy-eight arrived with their fathers in carriages creaking under roof-loads of bags, trunks, bedding, and clothing. Most of the girls came from New England but there were also girls from western New York, Pennsylvania, New Jersey, and far-off Cincinnati. One father brought four girls on a three-day journey from Vermont.

With each arrival Mary Lyon turned from her work of helping the men, her dirt-streaked face beaming with joy, "to give the welcome of a mother to her daughter."

The fathers of the pupils were pressed into service, to unload carriages, set up furniture, and tack down matting.

At four o'clock a bell was rung. The girls and their fathers gathered in the large hall. Mount Holyoke was proclaimed in session.

"This is an experiment," Mary Lyon told her girls, "and I cannot succeed without your help. The life of the institution depends upon this first year."

There were hardships the first year, inadequate facilities and equipment, a struggle for funds. Miss Caldwell's health failed and she left for a lengthy vacation. Mary Lyon took over her duties.

But all the difficulties vanished from her mind in the joy of the first commencement, on August 23, 1838, following two days of public examination in the seminary hall before an admiring audience.

On a bright Thursday afternoon the white-gowned students, led by the principal in a new dress of lavender, walked in solemn procession to the village church. Wrote Miss Caldwell, who had returned for the occasion:

"The side pews and galleries were already crowded with interested spectators when Miss Lyon led her beautiful troop in quiet dignity to the seats reserved for them.

"It was an hour in her life never to be forgotten. The battle had been fought, the victory was hers . . ."

Three seniors bore away graduation certificates—Sarah Brigham, Abigail Moore, Persis Woods, the first of an unending procession of the daughters of Mary Lyon.

For twelve years Mary Lyon guided and built Mount Holyoke. Buildings were added. Equipment, a library and a laboratory were acquired. In numbers of students it compared favorably with New England's men's colleges. It expanded to the proportions that Mary Lyon had planned for it.

She died then as she had lived, in devotion to her daughters. Her once robust health weakened by years of prodigious labors, she arose from bed, to which she had been confined by a cold, to care for a senior fatally ill with erysipelas, and contracted the disease herself.

She died on March 5, 1849. She was fifty-two years old.

Her death, wrote one student, was "like the blotting of the sun out of the heavens at midday." The news traveled throughout the world and to thousands in many lands it brought a sense of loss.

Her remains were laid at rest on a slope east of the seminary building, at the foot of an oak tree. Dr. Herman Humphrey, ex-president of Amherst College, conducted the funeral service. He said:

"Her life was a shining path."

Susan B. Anthony

HER NAME is Susan Brownell Anthony and she looks out upon the world from a monument in the National Capitol in Washington. Washington is a good place for her to be. Things happen there.

Things like the adoption of the Nineteenth Amendment to the Constitution—the Susan B. Anthony Amendment, it was called—which gave women the vote in 1920.

Like President Franklin D. Roosevelt's appointment of Frances Perkins to be Secretary of Labor—the first woman Cabinet officer.

Or like the announcement of the Department of Labor two decades later that women had demonstrated they could do any work men could, because women were engaged in all 446 occupations listed by the Bureau of Census.

Susan B. Anthony fought for these advances. For more than a half century she fought. She was the leader, the voice, the inspiration of the woman's rights movement.

She was thirty-three when she made her first talk for woman's rights, a tall, straight-backed schoolteacher with luxurious brown hair and warm blue eyes. She made it in the summer of 1853 in the city of Rochester, New York.

Susan Anthony was participating at the time in the annual convention of the New York State Teachers Association. It was an odd kind of participation by present-day standards, for she was just listening and observing. But that is what society then expected of a woman at a public gathering—that is, when she was permitted to attend at all.

Women made up two-thirds of the membership of the Association, but until Susan spoke not one had ever opened her mouth at a convention except to yawn or whisper a remark to another woman.

The men, the minority, did all the speaking and voting.

For two days Susan had sat on a hard chair, struggling to contain a rising anger while man after man spoke complainingly of the poor salaries paid teachers. Her fingernails dug into her palms in vexation. Couldn't these men see the why and the wherefore of this? How could they be so blind?

A man who had been speaking for twenty minutes without saying anything new spread his coattails and sat down, and the presiding officer scanned the hall for other men who wished to speak. Apparently there were none. He was about to utter the words closing the discussion when she jumped to her feet.

"Mr. President," she said.

The presiding officer, Charles Davies, professor of mathematics at the United States Military Academy, regarded her blankly. "What will the lady have?" he asked.

"The lady," she said in a voice which emerged firm despite her inner quavering, "wishes to speak to the question under discussion."

Susan Anthony heard mutters of protest, snickers and a

hiss of "shame." Susan looked straight ahead at the presiding officer in military uniform, reading the indecision in his face.

Davies tapped with his gavel for silence. The delegates would have to rule on this astonishing request. "What is the pleasure of the convention?" he asked.

A debate began. It lasted for a half hour; all the speakers were men. At length Davies put the issue to vote and by a narrow margin—with only men voting—Susan Anthony was given the floor.

She turned so as to face rows of chairs where the men were seated, clasping her hands together to hide their trembling. She spoke in a rich contralto voice.

"For two days you have deplored the fact that the profession of teacher is not so highly respected as that of lawyer, doctor, or minister. It seems to me that you fail to comprehend the cause of the disrespect of which you complain.

"Do you not see"—a note of anger entered her voice—"that so long as society says that a woman has not brains enough to be a lawyer, doctor, or minister but has plenty to be a teacher, every one of you who condescends to teach admits before Israel and the sun that he has no more brains than a woman?"

She sank to her chair. The convention sat hushed. Only the scratching of the secretary's pen racing to catch up with her words could be heard. At length a male teacher moved that the convention be recessed for the day. The men seemed to greet the motion with relief and voted it approval.

Susan Anthony walked to the door. Women went to join her, to express thanks for her remarks. But some women drew aside their skirts and turned their backs at her approach.

That evening Susan and a newly gained supporter, a Mrs. Northrop, worked on a resolution which would pledge the New York State Teachers Association to recognize "the rights of female teachers to share in all the privileges and deliberations of this body."

The next morning Mrs. Northrop, clutching Susan by the hand, asked for the floor. Recognized by the chairman, she read the resolution. The majority of women voted for it, and some men. The resolution carried.

It was Susan Anthony's first small victory.

She was born February 15, 1820, in Adams, Massachusetts, a pleasant village of white-painted dwellings tucked away in the Berkshire hills.

Many of the inhabitants of Adams were Quakers, and her father, Daniel Anthony, was himself a member of the Society of Friends. This was important in the upbringing of the child, for the Society of Friends was the first religious sect to extend equality to its women members.

When Susan was old enough to go to Quaker meeting she heard women express their views in public discussion and vote. She even saw her father's mother, Mrs. Hannah Anthony, sit on the high seat as an elder of the meeting.

To most men this was further evidence that the Quakers, with their drab garments and "thee and thou" speech, were a queer lot. By their standards Daniel was even queerer.

He believed that women were the equals of men in brains and ability. Daniel, the owner of a small cotton mill, raised four daughters and two sons. He raised them as equals. In his eyes the girls were different from the boys—different, not inferior.

Susan, the second eldest of the Anthony children, was her father's favorite. The tall, intelligent Quaker loved to hold her in his arms before bedtime and observe her eyes grow round with wonder as he told of dangerous exploration in the West, of the wonders of scientific discovery, of exciting developments in manufacture.

The child imagined herself playing starring roles in these wonderful tales, not knowing that in real life such were reserved for the male sex.

Like other girls, Susan was raised with the outlook that she would marry and have children. Her mother trained her well in household tasks, teaching her to cook and preserve food, to keep a spotless house, to spin and weave, to cut and sew clothes. As a woman Susan was a model housekeeper and an excellent cook whose dishes were the delight of her friends.

Susan's mother was not a happy woman. A non-Quaker, Lucy Read Anthony before her marriage was a happy, laughing girl, the belle of Adams. In marrying a Friend, she was compelled to put away her gay dresses and attire herself in the mud-colored clothes of Quaker women; to give up singing and dancing, which she loved.

Lucy Anthony's personality changed after her marriage. She became withdrawn and anxious. She spoke little.

As a child, Susan loved and pitied her mother. Sensing Lucy's hunger for the pretty things she once possessed, the child would save money given her by her father and grandparents and buy for her mother a bit of embroidery, a delicate cup and saucer, or a string of beads.

But often Susan was outspokenly critical of Mrs. Anthony. Once Lucy reprimanded her for staying at Grandmother Read's for supper, when the same supper was awaiting her at home. Susan replied saucily, "Why, Grand-mother's potato peelings are better than your boiled dinners."

Another incident involving Mrs. Anthony left Susan with an anger which endured for years.

When Susan was nearly four she was sent with her elder sister Guelma to Grandmother Anthony's to stay during the birth of Lucy's fourth child. The two little girls re-mained six weeks with their grandmother and during this time they had whooping cough and learned to read.

Susan raced home at the end of the visit and excitedly told her mother that she could read—"real words in books!" Lucy, whose baby had been born dead, didn't hear a word. Shocked, she stared at Susan's eyes which had turned in toward her nose during the illness, and wrung her hands in anguish. Lucy acted as if having crossed eyes was a dis-grace.

In time Susan's left eye corrected itself and her right be-came almost normal. But she remained convinced all her life that her eyes were markedly crossed, causing strangers to stare. As a woman she refused for many years to pose for full view portraits; she believed that they would show up her crossed eyes.

Daniel gave his daughters a good education in a time when women were not permitted to enter college. Susan and Guelma attended village school in Adams. When Susan was six the family moved to Battenville, New York, some forty miles to the northwest, where Daniel had acquired a larger mill. In Battenville he established a small private school which his children attended. In their early teens Susan and Guelma had a private tutor and later they studied at a Quaker finishing school near Philadelphia.

Daniel also taught his children himself. By word and example he instructed them in a simple religion and a way of life.

He taught them to love God. And one shows his love of God, he would say, by loving humanity. This he translated to mean working, speaking, sacrificing for human betterment.

His creed led him into many reform movements. He was a tireless worker against slavery and a force in the temperance movement. Himself a liberal employer, he spoke for good wages and working conditions for workers.

"Tolerate not evil against humanity," he would tell his children. "And when thee is powerless to do anything else, speak with vigor. Protest!"

Susan was five when she witnessed her first demonstration of protest.

As a Quaker Daniel was opposed to war and did not want to pay taxes to a government which upheld force of arms as an instrument of state policy. However, he could not escape paying his taxes so he resorted to a formula which would express his feelings about the matter.

He took Susan by the hand one day and walked with her to the home of the tax collector. There he laid his purse on the table and said, "I shall not voluntarily pay these taxes. But if thee wants to steal from my purse thou can do so." Gravely the tax collector counted out the money due the government and returned Daniel his purse.

Daniel taught his children well.

Before the Civil War broke out his son Jacob went to Kansas and enlisted in the antislavery guerrilla band of John Brown, taking part in the historical raid on Osawatomie.

His other son, Daniel Read, followed his younger brother to Kansas to fight and stayed on to become a reform-minded newspaper publisher and mayor of Leavenworth.

His daughters Guelma, Hannah, and Mary became abolitionists, worked for temperance and joined the Woman's Rights Movement when it was formed.

And Susan—Susan was her father's best pupil.

At eighteen she was a happy, eager girl, her body slim and athletic. Her features were pleasing, showing the promise of later handsomeness. She had her fair share of boy friends, with whom she went on picnics and buggy rides. In her diary she jotted many notes about the boys who were her friends:

"Job Whipple and William Norton called here last night and made quite a little visit. I had very good times . . . I awoke this morning a little after midnight and went to the window and saw the constellation Libra and some others, which so filled my mind with the beauty of the stars that I could not get to sleep."

Another note tells that "R. Wilson" sent her "a piece of poetry on love."

Susan was convinced, however, that she was homely—and cross-eyed—and one item in her diary reveals her belief that she could not compete with physical attractiveness for a boy's attention.

"Job is at Marie Wilson's," she wrote. "May he know that he has found in me a spirit congenial to his own and not suffer the glare of beauty to attract both eye and heart."

The pleasant secure life at home ended suddenly for Susan in 1838. Daniel Anthony, who had stretched his credit to the utmost to expand his Battenville business, was forced into bankruptcy in the worst economic depression the young nation had ever experienced.

Creditors seized everything—the Battenville mill, the family home, furniture, silverware, household utensils and linens. Many of the things were Lucy's, the gifts of her parents, but these were taken too. Under the law a wife owned nothing. Everything she had was her husband's and could be seized in payment for his debts.

It became imperative that the two oldest children, Guelma and Susan, go to work to support themselves and help their father. They found employment as teachers, Guelma near home and Susan at a girls' boarding school in New Rochelle, New York.

In growing up, Susan had perceived that the world's treatment of women was different from what she was used to at home and in Quaker meeting. She proceeded now to learn by experience how great that difference was.

She spent the greater part of the next fifteen years as a teacher. At the outset she was better equipped through education than most teachers of her time, men and women. Then while teaching she studied hard to improve herself, to become expert in subjects neglected in her own schooling.

Susan taught in a half-dozen schools, public and private. Her first position paid $2 a week, minus $1 a week for board. The most she ever earned was $3, out of which $1 weekly was taken for board. This summit of earnings was achieved at Canajoharie Academy, in Canajoharie, New York, where she was employed as headmistress of the girls' department. It was a much-sought-after position.

As the years passed it angered her more and more. Not the money—money never meant much to her. But money paid in salary was a measure of worth, and her greatest worth was $3 a week. A male teacher was paid three times as much.

She had a strong need to progress. She believed she was able and she yearned to undertake tasks worthy of her ability. But there was no opportunity for a woman of ability, she learned. A woman could be a teacher, a governess, a seamstress, a servant, a factory hand, a barmaid—little else.

Ever since leaving Battenville Susan had taken a small part in reform, chiefly in work against slavery and strong drink. At Canajoharie, where she went at the age of twenty-six, she became more active.

She joined the Canajoharie Daughters of Temperance and was elected president. She planned various activities, got them approved by the members and then directed their execution. They were usually successful. The organization achieved a local influence.

The work gratified her. She was achieving, finding an outlet for ideas and energies, progressing—and in doing these things she was also helping people. An exciting purpose began to form in her mind—to make a career in reform.

Susan discussed it in letters to her family. Her father approved heartily. He urged her to come home to live, and offered financial help because she could not expect to earn a living in reform. Daniel, who had suffered several setbacks in his struggle to reestablish himself, had at this time a good position with an insurance company in Rochester, New York.

Susan was teaching in Canajoharie when the first Woman's Rights convention was held in Seneca Falls, New York, on July 19 and 20, 1848. She read about it in the Canajoharie newspaper which reported that sixty-eight women and thirty-two men had signed their names to a Declaration of

Woman's Rights demanding for women free education, equality of opportunity in industry and the professions, free speech, the right to take part in public affairs and the right to vote.

Reading, she nodded her head in approval. This was excellent! Yet she did not feel moved to join the new Woman's Rights Movement. It was more important, she reasoned, to give her services to the abolitionist and temperance causes. Nearly five years were to elapse before she changed her mind, or rather narrow-minded men changed it for her.

In the fall of 1849 she began carrying out her plan for a reform career. She went to Rochester to live in the family's new home. She taught school for a while in the Rochester area but gradually ceased this work to give all her time to reform, particularly to temperance.

She found in Rochester a small Daughters of Temperance group and breathed vitality into it. Then she traveled about the nearby towns and villages, speaking to women about the need to curb the sale of liquor and organizing them in lodges of the Daughters of Temperance.

She was content. She felt she had found her place in life.

While she was organizing the women, she worked to obtain official recognition of the Daughters by the men's organization, the Sons of Temperance. Such recognition, she hoped, would be followed by a union of the two organizations.

She reasoned that without the men the women could not be very effective. Their lodges were few and women had no money of their own to give to organizing activities. More important, legislators paid little heed to the women's lodges because their members could not vote.

In time Susan established a state-wide organization of women's temperance groups but the men refused to recognize them. In her efforts to obtain this recognition Susan was several times harshly rebuffed.

These rebuffs prompted her to reexamine her decision to work for temperance and the abolition of slavery, and not for woman's rights. Was she making a mistake? Did women have to win all their own rights before they could work usefully in reform?

In her work for temperance Susan often collaborated with the leaders of the woman's rights movement—Mrs. Elizabeth Cady Stanton, Mrs. Lucretia Mott, pretty Lucy Stone. They sought to convince her that the answer to her questions was "yes." But they weren't successful until Susan had had a few more experiences with the men's temperance organization. The most humiliating of these occurred at Syracuse, New York.

A state convention of the New York State Sons of Temperance was scheduled to be held in Syracuse and the local lodge, as sponsor of the gathering, invited the women's state organization to send delegates. Susan and Mrs. Amelia Bloomer were appointed.

On their arrival in Syracuse the two women were met by a clergyman who said he had been delegated to inform them that the convention had rescinded the invitation of the Syracuse lodge. Susan and Mrs. Bloomer told the spokesman that they had come to Syracuse by invitation to attend the convention and attend they would. But they never bargained for the violent attack which was provoked by their entrance into the convention hall.

The two women were ordered by the chairman to leave.

They were hooted at, jeered at. One man arose and declared that no business would be transacted until "these creatures, a hybrid species, half-man and half-woman, belonging to neither sex, are put out."

The women departed, trembling with wrath and shock. A short time later plump Mrs. Stanton said to Susan, "Do you see now?" Susan answered sadly, "My eyes are open. I see at last."

The Susan Anthony who began working for woman's rights was at thirty-three a poised and mature woman, well-read, well-informed.

She dressed in quiet good taste, being especially fond of a dress of gray silk with pale blue ribbons. Such a dress was frowned on by the Quakers but ever since her Canajoharie days Susan had been disregarding the Friends' severe rules of dress and deportment. At Canajoharie she had dropped the singular speech of the Quakers—the "thee" speech— and even learned to dance.

Stately, with a handsomely shaped head over which her thick brown hair was tightly drawn, she attracted all eyes at gatherings. Her expression was warm and friendly, her generous mouth usually curved in a smile. Men seeing her for the first time whispered that here was "a fine figure of a woman."

The only one who did not believe this was Susan herself. She thought of herself as an unattractive woman with crossed eyes. She persisted in this view of herself even though a number of men asked her to marry them.

She turned down all the men who proposed, always finding a reason to justify herself. One well-to-do widower, who said she reminded him of his first wife, pursued her at great length. Giggling, Susan told her friends that she wouldn't marry him because she "didn't intend to become a second."

To the woman's rights movement Susan brought a great gift. This was a talent for organizing and leading, developed in several years' work for temperance. To her, weaknesses of the movement were quickly apparent.

Talking with Mrs. Stanton, who became her dearest friend, she stressed that it wasn't enough to give speeches and write leaflets about woman's rights. The movement needed a permanent functioning organization. It needed members by the thousands and the way to get them was to go where women were to be found, in their own homes. And it needed, she declared, a program of immediate action which would attract members and give them tasks to do.

Mrs. Stanton approved of Susan's ideas and her intention of carrying them out. In the fall of 1853, following her first talk for woman's rights at the teachers convention in Rochester, Susan began to work.

Paying her own expenses with funds provided by her father, she set out on a tour of western New York State. She called on housewives in the towns and villages and told them about the movement and its Declaration of Rights.

She made many converts and organized them in groups. A large number of women, however, became angry or scornful when Susan explained her mission and ordered her from their homes. Some said cuttingly that they didn't need laws to give them rights—*they* had husbands to look after them.

En route home on a jolting soot-coated train, Susan thought long about further steps in her organizational campaign and developed a plan. There would be a state convention of the local groups which would prepare a demand for woman's rights to be submitted to the State Legislature.

With Susan attending to all the preparations, a well-attended convention was held in Rochester. Her proposal for an approach to the Legislature was approved, and she was elected unanimously to organize the project.

From among the new members Susan appointed a number of aides. Then during the winter of 1853–54 Susan and these women trudged from house to house collecting signatures to petitions requesting that married women be granted the right to their own earnings and property, to enter into contracts, to sue and be sued, to be equal guardians with their husbands of minor children, and to vote.

Ten thousand signatures were obtained and two bills embodying the intent of the petitions were introduced before the Legislature in Albany. In both the Assembly and the Senate, the bills and petitions were ridiculed and attacked. Typical were the words of Assemblyman Burnett:

"Are we going to give the least countenance to claims so preposterous, disgraceful, and criminal? Are we to put the stamp of truth upon the libel here set forth that men and women in their matrimonial relations are to be equal? We *know* that God created man as the representative of the race."

Both houses rejected the bills by overwhelming majorities. The women sitting in the galleries were discouraged. Not Susan. Grimly she told the legislators in the corridors, "We will be back. We will be back again and again until the laws are enacted giving women their due rights."

She had the tenacity of a bulldog. During the spring,

summer, and fall she worked at organizing more groups
and collecting signatures to the petitions. To climax her
campaign she determined to give lectures in as many of the
State's sixty counties as possible.

With her father guaranteeing payment, she went into
debt for several thousand handbills advertising her lectures
and sent them out to sheriffs and postmasters with letters
asking that the handbills be prominently displayed.

Then with fifty dollars in cash and a carpetbag bulging
with petitions she left Rochester by train on Christmas
Day, 1854, on the start of her tour.

In her diary Susan recorded her experiences during the
coldest and snowiest New York winter in ten years. In some
towns she had well-attended meetings and her appeals for
contributions met a good response. In other towns she was
refused the use of church or schoolhouse to talk about the
"detestable woman's doctrine." When this occurred she
visited women in their homes, then traveled on to the
next town by sleigh.

In the town of Olean she was able to hold a meeting only
because the owner of the hotel offered his dining room. She
noted that a young minister signed her petition, then hastily
crossed off his name when a wealthy parishioner threatened
to leave his church.

She stopped working in February to go to Albany with an
armload of petitions to the Legislature. But none of the
members of the Legislature would introduce a woman's
rights bill. She wouldn't quit, but went off to the freezing
Lake George and Schroon Lake districts for more meetings
and signatures to be used the following year.

Often when snowstorms slowed her passage from one

town to another she went hungry. Her hands and feet became frostbitten. Each night in a cold village inn she would soak them in cold water. Her back began to ache; the pain became agonizing and she had to bite her lips to keep from groaning. But she plodded on.

The first of May Susan returned home, thin as a lath, her body one whole ache. But triumphant. She had lectured and obtained signatures in fifty-four counties. She had collected $2,367, spent $2,291 and had $76 remaining.

Her father urged her to keep the surplus and buy herself some new dresses, for she was still wearing the clothes purchased in Canajoharie. "No," she said, "that will be for next year's campaign."

The next year's campaign didn't move the legislators, nor the one after that. Seven times Susan and her woman's righters went before the Legislature. On their seventh appearance they were successful. In March of 1860 the Legislature adopted a bill giving married women the right to their own earnings and property, to sue and be sued, to enter into contracts, and to be equal guardians with their husbands of their minor children.

It was the first break in the thousand-year-old English common law restricting the rights of women. The credit belonged mostly to Susan Anthony.

Soon the Civil War began. Daniel Anthony, convinced that only through war could slavery be eliminated, voted for the first time, casting a ballot for Abraham Lincoln. Before the war was over he was dead, a victim of what the doctors termed "neuralgia of the stomach."

Susan grieved over the death of her father, but while she grieved she worked. With Mrs. Stanton she organized the

Woman's National Loyal League which rallied women in support of the Union, emancipation of the slaves, and woman's rights.

The war over, Susan returned to woman's rights work, proclaiming, "Still another form of slavery remains to be disposed of."

Her reputation grew and reached to every corner of the land. She was much in demand as a lecturer. Supporting herself by her fees, she traveled throughout the country, speaking on woman's rights.

In a year it was not unusual for her to speak in two hundred communities strung from the Atlantic to the Pacific. The physical strain of travel, particularly in the sparsely settled Middle and Far West, was terrific.

In order to reach her destinations on schedule she often had to take trains at all hours of the night. Sometimes the only train available was a freight and she rode squeezed in with bags of flour, cases of shoes, tools, and rifles. Many times she had to ride cross-country for twenty-five or thirty miles in a lumber wagon or an open buggy in snow and rain.

On the western frontiers she slept in dirty, unheated rooms, often the only woman in crude inns where men drank and reveled throughout the night at the bar. For weeks at a time she lived on a diet of soggy bread and dried meat.

Only one frontier hardship she found intolerable—the bedbug. Once in Kansas she went four days and nights without sleep "because our tormentors were so active." Even though she plucked thousands of bedbugs from her hair and the seams of her clothing, enough remained undetected to cover every square inch of her body with bites.

She won thousands of women to her cause, and many

men. But no woman in the history of America was more savagely attacked, scorned, and slandered for her ideas.

Drunken men threatened her with guns. Men made hideous effigies of her and burned them. Once acid was thrown at her—fortunately it burned only her garments.

The newspaper Syracuse Star described her as "a brawling woman and an atheist," and the New York World said, "Susan Anthony is lean, cadaverous, and intellectual, with the proportions of a file and the voice of a hurdy-gurdy."

In a piece of doggerel which became popular in the saloons she was depicted as usually half-clad, immoral, and smoking a big black cigar. She was accused of advocating polygamy and "free love."

She learned to endure the lies and attacks in silence. Sometimes, however, she was stung into a reply. An instance of this occurred at a convention of the New York State Teachers Association as she was leaving the meeting hall after making a brief talk. A teacher, a man of about fifty-five, detained her and said, "That was a magnificent statement, Miss Anthony. But I must tell you that I would rather see my wife or daughter in her coffin than hear her speaking as you did, before a public assembly."

Susan's eyes flashed in anger for a moment. Then she said quietly, "Sir, I wonder if the ladies of your family agree with you that their deaths are to be preferred to speaking for dignity and opportunity."

On another occasion the target of her retort was Horace Greeley, the famous newspaper publisher and editor. Susan was urging a committee of the New York State Legislature to approve a proposal giving women the vote when the round-faced Greeley, the committee chairman, interrupted her.

"Miss Anthony," he drawled, "you are aware that the ballot and the bullet go together. If you vote are you also prepared to fight?"

She answered sweetly, "Certainly, Mr. Greeley. Just as you fought in the Civil War—at the point of a goose quill."

Increasingly the woman's rights forces began to stress the ballot, suffrage, as their key demand. Women would gain their full rights only when they were enfranchised, the leaders of the movement declared.

Susan and the other leaders repeatedly urged Congress to initiate a Constitutional amendment spelling out the right of women to vote. Simultaneously many of the women began to support a theory that under the Fourteenth Amendment, adopted to confer the ballot on Negroes, women were already entitled to the ballot. These women emphasized that in the Fourteenth Amendment Congress for the first time defined a citizen as any person born or naturalized in the United States. The amendment made no mention of sex.

Susan was not among the first to adopt this theory but once she adopted it she decided to act. The result was one of the most daring political coups in American history.

On November 1, 1872, Susan appeared at a shoemaker's shop on West Street in Rochester at the head of fifteen women. The shop was the polling headquarters for the city's eighth ward. Susan informed the dumbfounded election inspectors, "We are here to be enrolled as voters."

When the inspectors declared that "women can't vote—it's illegal" she produced from a capacious pocketbook a copy of the United States Constitution and challenged the men to prove it. Uneasily the inspectors enrolled all sixteen women, among them Susan's sisters, Miss Mary Anthony,

Mrs. Guelma Anthony McLean, and Mrs. Hannah Anthony Mosher.

Four days later, Election Day, the same sixteen women returned to the shoemaker's shop and voted after Susan had once more disposed of the inspectors' objections.

The Anthony coup was reported in the newspapers of the land in heavy black type. At the same time newspapers published angry editorials demanding the arrest and imprisonment of Susan B. Anthony and her associates as lawbreakers.

If Miss Anthony got away with it, the editorials emphasized, she would by a single pencil mark on her ballot have enfranchised every woman in America.

The administration of President Ulysses S. Grant in Washington appreciated the danger and determined on the prosecution of the Rochester women.

On Thanksgiving Day a United States marshal in top hat rang the bell of the Anthony home in Rochester. Susan came to the door and the marshal, flushed with embarrassment, produced a warrant for Susan's arrest.

The marshal said that to spare herself embarrassment Miss Anthony could go to the courthouse without him, but she said, "Oh dear, no. I much prefer to be taken, handcuffed if possible."

The officer indignantly refused to supply handcuffs but he did escort Susan to the courthouse where she found waiting the fifteen other culprits and an attorney she had engaged in anticipation of trouble. Her attorney was Henry B. Selden, a scholarly veteran of the courts who had agreed to act for her after some twenty other lawyers had turned her down.

Presented before an elections commissioner, all sixteen

women pleaded not guilty to a charge of voting illegally in a national election and were ordered held in $500 bail each.

Fifteen put up bail. Susan refused and demanded her release on a writ of habeas corpus. A hearing on her request was subsequently held in the federal court in Albany and it was turned down. In Albany her bail was increased to $1,000. Once more she refused to provide bail.

The militant Quakeress would have been remanded to jail pending the start of her trial had not Selden put up bail without her knowledge. "I could not see a lady go to jail," he apologized to Susan.

The trial of the sixteen women was set for the summer of 1873 in Rochester. Susan decided that inasmuch as she had instigated the voting it was only proper that she should pay all the costs of the trial. However, on her return to Rochester from the Albany hearing she had exactly $13 in the bank. Although many woman's rights groups adopted resolutions praising the courage of the Rochester voters, not one donated as much as a dollar for the expense of the trial.

Susan decided to go on a lecture tour. By this means she would raise money and utilize the great national interest in the trial to educate men and women about woman's rights.

She toured the Midwest, speaking on the subject "Is It a Crime for a United States Citizen to Vote?" Everywhere she was heard by large and enthusiastic audiences. The tour was a success.

But Susan was fifty-three now and the strain of constant travel, added to the tension caused by the forthcoming trial, exhausted her. Midway through her talk in Fort Wayne, Indiana, one night she collapsed.

A doctor summoned to treat her at the home of a friend in Fort Wayne instructed Susan sternly to return home at once for a long rest. She took his advice to the extent of going home, arriving with $218 left over after paying travel expenses. Of this she gave Selden $215.

She rested for a brief period—rested her body, that is. Her mind worked energetically. The trial would be held in Rochester, the seat of Monroe County. Thus all the jurors would have to be residents of the county. Good! She would lecture throughout the county and inform everyone within reach of her voice of the issues.

She set out on this new tour. Speaking on twenty-nine nights in one month, she covered every one of Monroe County's post-office districts. After each talk she asked her audience to vote on whether she had broken the law. By large majorities the people voted that she had not broken the law and many men came forward to pledge that if they were chosen to serve on the jury they would vote to acquit her.

The government, meanwhile, was making its own preparations for the trial. United States Senator Roscoe Conkling, President Grant's right hand man and Republican boss of New York State, was appointed to direct the government's behind-the-scenes strategy.

The first development of this strategy was a decision to try only Susan B. Anthony, the "Woman Napoleon," as the newspapers called her.

The government wanted a conviction in the case to smash the threat that women would be enfranchised and Conkling believed it would be easier to convict the detested Anthony woman than a group of sixteen women, most of them housewives whose names had never appeared in the newspapers.

A second development was a request made of the court by the prosecutor to transfer Susan Anthony's trial from Monroe County to adjoining Ontario County. The request was made, the prosecutor said, because Miss Anthony by her marathon lecture series had "corrupted" the citizens of Monroe County.

The request was granted and a trial date of June 17 was set for the little town of Canandaigua. But before the trial could begin Susan "corrupted" the citizens of Ontario County too. In three weeks she spoke in twenty-one districts of the county and Mrs. Matilda Gage, another woman's rights leader, in sixteen.

The case of the government versus Susan B. Anthony opened on a pleasant June day to the tolling of a bell in the Canandaigua courthouse. To Susan it appeared to be tolling a warning.

Judge Nathan Hall, known as a severe but fair-minded jurist, was to have presided at her trial; but in his place sat another man. In the courthouse, packed with members of the woman's movement, notables, and newspaper reporters, it was whispered that Judge Hall had "refused to take orders."

The prim, thin-lipped man in black broadcloth seated on the bench was the Honorable Ward Hunt, Associate Justice of the United States Supreme Court. The reporters scribbled furiously. A Justice of the Supreme Court assigned to try a case in the Circuit Court.

The politically wise in the courtroom, and Susan, too, were sure that they knew the explanation for the assignment of Justice Hunt. The government intended to make certain that Susan Anthony was found guilty. Judge Hunt only recently had been appointed to the High Court through the influence of his friend Senator Conkling, and this was his first trial. He naturally felt under strong obligation to the man who had managed his appointment, it was thought.

The trial which all America was watching was brief. It required only two days.

The prosecuting attorney outlined the case against the defendant. Then Attorney Selden asked that his client be summoned to the stand to testify in her defense.

Judge Hunt turned down the request. The defendant, he explained, was not competent to testify—she was a woman.

As Selden protested and Susan bit her lips in anger, Judge Hunt added suavely that he would act for the defendant by reading the testimony she gave at her hearing. This he proceeded to do.

All the evidence had now been submitted in this mockery of a trial. The prosecutor made a brief, almost careless, summation. And Selden delivered a lengthy and passionate defense. Except for one further action the trial was over. It came now from Judge Hunt.

He drew from his pocket a sheet of paper, unfolded it and began to read. It was a charge to the jury and, hearing it, Susan shot to her feet in angry agitation.

Judge Hunt declared that Susan had voted illegally and was not protected by the Constitution against the consequences of her act. Then he told the jury with slow deliberation:

". . . the result must be a verdict on your part of guilty, and I therefore direct that you find a verdict of guilty."

The outraged Selden protested that by directing the jury

to submit a finding of guilty Judge Hunt was acting with serious irregularity. Ignoring him, Judge Hunt impatiently instructed the clerk of the court, "Take the verdict." The clerk mumbled:

"Gentlemen of the jury, hearken to your verdict as the court has recorded it. You say you find the defendant guilty of the offense whereof she stands indicted, and so say you all."

The jurymen had not said anything of the kind, but merely sat in embarrassed silence while the words were put in their mouths.

After the clerk had recited his formula and entered the verdict Judge Hunt said, "Gentlemen of the jury, you are discharged."

The trial was over.

Susan Anthony appeared in court again the next day to receive sentence. Her anger was under control and to those in the courtroom, aware that they were onlookers in a great moment in history, she appeared calm and poised. Selden bit his nails anxiously. He knew that his client could be fined $500 and sentenced to prison for three years.

Judge Hunt rapped the court to order, then ordered the defendant to rise. Now that the trial was over he felt that he could permit her to say a few words. "Has the prisoner anything to say why sentence should not be pronounced?" he asked.

Susan, gagged during the trial, hadn't dreamed that she would be permitted to speak at this time, hadn't prepared anything. But as a veteran of twenty years on the lecture platform she was ready.

Her voice rang out in the courtroom.

"Yes, Your Honor, I have many things to say, for in your ordered verdict of guilty you have trampled underfoot every vital principle of our government. My natural rights, my civil rights, my political rights are all ignored. Robbed of the fundamental privilege of citizenship, I am degraded from the status of citizen to that of subject; and not only myself individually but all of my sex are by Your Honor's verdict doomed to political subjection."

Judge Hunt realized his mistake. Every word uttered by the stately woman in black silk was being taken down by the reporters and would be spread before the eyes of the nation. He interrupted her, "The court cannot listen to a—"

Her trained speaker's voice rose above his, uttering facts, arguments:

". . . all my prosecutors, from the eighth ward corner grocer politician who entered the complaint, to the United States marshal, commissioner, district attorney, district judge, Your Honor on the bench, not one is my peer, but each and all my political sovereigns. And had Your Honor submitted my case to the jury, as was clearly your duty, even then I should have had just cause for protest, for not one of these men was my peer; but native or foreign, white or black, rich or poor, educated or ignorant, awake or asleep, sober or drunk, each and every man of them was my political superior."

"The prisoner," the Judge shouted, "will sit down!"

She ignored him, continued. Unable to cope with her, Judge Hunt was goaded into making a defense. "The prisoner," he shouted, "has been tried according to established forms of law."

Like the lash of a whip came her retort, "Yes, Your Honor,

but by forms of law made by men, interpreted by men, administered by men, in favor of men—and against women."

She resumed, ignoring the rapping of Judge Hunt's gavel, with her impassioned words ripping to shreds the case against her. She finished by saying that, failing to get justice or even a trial by jury, "I ask not leniency at your hands, but to take the full rigors of the law."

Judge Hunt, glaring with anger, pronounced sentence— a fine of $100 and court costs.

Again she was on her feet to declare, "I shall never pay a dollar of your unjust penalty."

And she never did. Nor did she go to prison for her refusal, because Judge Hunt in imposing sentence had deliberately refrained from adding the customary formula that the prisoner be sent to jail until the fine was paid.

Had he done this Susan Anthony would have gone to jail and could have taken her case directly to the Supreme Court on a writ of habeas corpus.

The years passed and every year Susan Anthony gave 365 days to the cause of woman's advancement. And women were advancing. In time four states enacted legislation giving them the vote. Women and girls were entering college in increasing numbers; new colleges for women were being founded.

When she was in New York City Susan was fond of rising early and visiting the business sections to observe women and girls going to work in stores, in offices, occasionally even in professional surroundings.

To millions of women the erect Quakeress with the whitening hair was the symbol of the new progress. Many prayed for her, but when one woman confessed this to Susan she became angry. "Pray with your hands and feet," she said. "I like prayers that take the form of work."

She was even angrier when she learned that some women had taken to calling her "Saint Anthony." "What rubbish!" she snapped.

Men, too, recognized her unselfish devotion and by the thousands they swung to support of her ideas and goals. All America began to appreciate that she was one of the greatest Americans of the nation's history.

Her name became an inspiration throughout the world. Dramatic evidence of this was given in Chicago in 1893 at the World's Congress of Representative Women, the first such conclave in history. Twenty-seven nations were represented in the Chicago Art Palace.

Only ten thousand people could be seated at a time, but all one hundred and fifty thousand who passed through the gates pleaded to speak to, to touch, or at least to see the woman who had inspired them, Susan B. Anthony.

And when she was introduced to speak, men and women climbed on their chairs, threw hats, gloves, and handkerchiefs in the air and cheered for ten minutes before she said a word.

After a half century of work for woman's rights she was as poor as when she began. Every cent she earned, every cent given to her, she used for her work, keeping only a pittance for living expenses. After her trial in Canandaigua men and women sent her money, from twenty-five-cent pieces to one gift of $62, adding up to about $1,000. She gave it all to the cause.

For several years she was the editor of a woman's rights magazine. It failed, and there were debts of $10,000. Susan told the creditors that she would pay every cent due them. It took her six years but she paid every debt. Virtually every newspaper in the land applauded her. Typical was the editorial comment in the Buffalo Express:

"She has paid her debts like a man. Like a man? Not so. Not one man in a thousand but would have 'laid down' and settled at ten or twenty cents on the dollar."

As the twentieth century neared, the movement laid greater and greater emphasis on an amendment to the Constitution which would give women the right to vote. Susan, in addition to lecturing and serving as president or other executive officer of the movement, worked vigorously to win over congressmen and presidents to support such an amendment.

With work, she told the younger women coming into the movement—it was now called the National American Suffrage Association—the amendment was sure to be adopted.

In 1900, aged eighty, she stepped down as president of the Association "because I want to see the organization in the hands of those who are to have its management in the future."

Almost to the last hour of her life, Susan worked for the cause of women.

Beginning about 1901, she gave considerable time to a campaign to induce the University of Rochester in the city where she lived to open its doors to women. In time the University's board of trustees agreed to do this if a sufficient endowment for women students were raised.

Susan saw to the appointment of a committee to solicit funds and went off to an International Suffrage Congress in Germany. Tired and ailing, she returned home to learn that her brother Daniel was dying in Kansas. Off to Kansas sped the eighty-five-year-old woman and her younger sister Mary to bid a last farewell to Daniel.

Returning once more to Rochester, Susan had a visitor, the woman secretary of the fund raising committee. This woman told her that the fund was $8,000 short of the quota and the stipulated time limit would expire the next afternoon.

Not even pausing to change her clothes, the old war horse went into action. Mary Anthony had written into her will a bequest of $2,000 to the University if women were admitted. "Mary, you have to give me that money now," Susan said.

Mary gave her the money and Susan began calling on merchants, bankers, industrialists, working until evening. All turned her down.

Still $6,000 short, she started out the next morning. The pastor of a church gave her $2,000. Friends made pledges. At three o'clock, still lacking $2,000, Susan made a desperation visit to a man she knew to be sympathetic to her cause although in modest circumstances. To her relief he pledged the final $2,000.

Her old heart pounding furiously, she raced to a meeting of the University board of trustees and announced completion of the endowment fund.

The chairman examined the names and pledges on her list and told her regretfully that the last pledge could not be accepted. The chairman did not believe that the man who made it had $2,000.

Susan sat stunned for a moment. "I must think," she told

herself. "I must think." Then, inspired, she stood up. "I will pledge my life insurance for $2,000," she said. "Will you accept it?"

Her pledge was accepted. She had won another victory for women, but at a high cost.

Three days later Mary found her unconscious in bed. Doctors said she had suffered a stroke and would never be fully well again. Another stroke was certain to follow but this might be deferred if she stopped all activity and lived as a semi-invalid.

This Susan refused to do when she had improved sufficiently to leave her sickbed. "The hammer may as well fall one time as another," she said.

Accompanied by a nurse, she began to attend meetings, to lecture occasionally. In March of 1906 she went to her last woman's rights meeting, a celebration of her 86th birthday in Washington. There she gave a brief talk ending with the words—the last she spoke on a public platform—"Failure is impossible."

The trip was too much for her enfeebled body. On her return home she fell ill and succumbed a few days later. The announcement of her death in the Rochester Quaker Journal was of a simplicity in keeping with the way she had lived:

"13th 3rd mo. 1906. Susan Brownell Anthony died this morning in the 87th year of her life at her home 17 Madison Street at 12:40 o'clock. Pneumonia the cause."

Belva Ann Lockwood

THE COLONISTS who came to America from England brought with them the language and customs of their mother country. They also brought the law. The English common law became the basic legal code of most American states.

This old English code was the legal authority for the inferior status of women. It declared: "Husband and wife are one and he is the one." It said the husband was the "baron" of the household.

The women who fought for equal rights for their sex hated these declarations. They fought to overturn them. But at least one leader in this fight was glad that they hadn't yet been overturned.

She was Belva Ann Lockwood, a pioneer of her sex in the law. The slender and attractive lawyer used to lecture a good deal, and one of her favorite anecdotes told of an occasion on which she was satisfied with the discriminatory principles:

Shortly after she was admitted to the bar of Washington, D.C., in 1873 she undertook to defend a penniless young woman who had been charged with resisting arrest and shooting a constable. The man's wound was fortunately slight.

The police had suspected that the woman's husband was a robber, and the constable had come to her home with a search warrant to look for stolen goods.

"The husband had fled," Mrs. Lockwood would tell her audience, "instructing his wife to refuse entrance to anyone, even the police. He gave her a pistol and told her to use it if necessary.

"When I talked to my client in the Washington jail after her arrest she was bewildered, frightened, and burdened with guilt. She was near hysteria. She wept that she wanted only to confess her guilt and be punished."

Mrs. Lockwood told how she calmed the woman, then instructed her on her rights under the law. "I advised her not to plead guilty," she said. "Also I explained to her that no one is compelled to testify against himself. Thus it would be best if she didn't take the witness stand. It would be up to the prosecution to prove its charges.

"I thought I had convinced her and helped her to control her emotions," Mrs. Lockwood said. "But in the course of the trial she burst into tears, ran to the witness stand and told the whole story, acknowledging her guilt, in spite of anything I could do.

"I was stunned," Mrs. Lockwood said. "When my client had stopped talking and I had to get up I didn't know what to say. I just looked at the jury. They were all men, of course. I thought bitterly that's what common law did—kept women off juries. But the thought of common law brought an inspiration. I knew what I was going to say.

"I said, 'Gentlemen of the jury, the laws must be enforced.

My client has committed the double offense of resisting an officer of the law and shooting a man. She has admitted it. The District of Columbia is under common law. That law says that a woman must obey her husband. My client's husband told her to load a gun and shoot the first person who tried to force his way into the house. She obeyed him.

" 'Gentlemen, I claim that the husband loaded the gun and shot the officer. I claim that you are not trying the right person. Surely you would not have a woman resist her husband?' "

She paused on the speaking platform until her audience had stopped laughing. "The jury," she said, "brought in a verdict of not guilty." Again there was laughter.

Concluding the anecdote, she said, "The judge, a crusty gentleman, said, 'When the next case is brought in I'll call a new jury, for the old one has just done a hard day's work.' "

Belva Lockwood was one of that company of dedicated women who fought during the second half of the nineteenth century and into the twentieth for the vote.

With Elizabeth Cady Stanton, Lucy Stone, and Lucretia Mott, she set women to thinking and organized them to struggle for equality. She spoke at meetings with Antoinette Brown, the first woman regularly ordained to the ministry in America. Susan Anthony, the tall Quakeress who led the equal rights movement for decades, was her friend.

Mrs. Lockwood dramatized the demand for equal rights by running for the Presidency, the first woman to do so. But mostly she helped the advance of women by her pioneering role in the law.

Frequently after she had given a talk some women of the audience would linger to ask advice or questions about her life. What induced her to join the fight for women's rights, they asked. What prompted her to try to become a lawyer in the face of prejudice and opposition?

She answered, "When I was a young widow in Royalton —I don't expect you to know, but that's a village in western New York—some good and well-meaning gentlemen gave me a lesson in the way of the world toward women. I have never forgotten that lesson. It set me to thinking.

"This is what happened. I wanted a position to support myself and my little girl. One day I . . ."

Her thoughts flew back to the familiar places. The village street. The smith's shop with its clanging of metal against metal. The general store smelling of cheese and coffee, the crackers in barrels, the shiny boots and shoes on the shelves, the bright calico and gingham which she liked to finger.

Four miles from the village of Royalton was the farmhouse where she was born, an event entered in the family Bible which lay on a hanging shelf in the kitchen, "Belva Ann Bennett—24 October, 1830."

It was this kitchen with its broad chimney place which most often came to mind when she thought of her childhood home. It was there that she and Rachel, the oldest of the five Bennett children, polished the pewter, helped with the cooking and baking, or sat knitting on a rocking bench. It was there that the family ate its meals, there that Belva did her school lessons.

The pleasures of her childhood were simple. A quilting bee or a gathering of the farm families at which the men and older boys built a barn for a newlywed couple while the women and girls prepared and served food. In winter a ride with her father in the horse-drawn sleigh with the other children while wind and frost turned her cheeks apple red.

And once an event of huge excitement. The Bennett family went to Buffalo for a visit. They traveled by Erie Canal packet and Belva slept in the women's quarters. Buffalo's bigness excited her—thirty thousand people congregated in a single community. In Buffalo she saw her first railroad train—a panting locomotive and two coaches.

Although her teachers in the district school often told Mr. Bennett that she was unusually intelligent, Belva was in general no different from the score or so other Royalton farm girls of her age. There was nothing in her behavior, nothing in the ideas she expressed, to indicate that here was one who would rebel against the role expected of women.

However, when she was fourteen she did give evidence of at least a little extra in the way of courage and determination. In the spring of the year she finished grade school. Most of her friends felt this much education was enough. But Belva wanted more schooling. She would like to attend Girls' Academy in Royalton, she told her father and mother. Mr. and Mrs. Bennett were not against the idea, they said. But they couldn't afford the tuition.

The village school conducted a summer session. Mainly it was for farm boys who had to remain away from classes during the spring planting. One day Belva put on a new blue gingham gown with ruffles and a knitted gray shawl and went to a meeting of the five trustees of Royalton and asked for a job teaching in the summer school.

Her recommendations from her teachers were excellent but John McNall, who owned the village tavern, was doubtful. "You're rather young," he said. "Do you think you can handle those big farm lads? Keep order?"

Up came her firm little chin. "I'm sure I can," she said.

They gave her the job and she taught for three summers, earning enough to study at the Academy for three years.

It was while she was attending the Academy that Uriah McNall, son of the tavern keeper, became her beau. Belva liked him because he was not only handsome and good but was also interested in the great events of the world.

Walking along Niagara Road, holding hands, Belva and Uriah talked of the evils of slavery, Samuel Morse and his magnetic telegraph, and the westward expansion of the United States. Of course, they also talked of themselves and their feelings for each other. They fell in love.

At the age of eighteen, pretty, fair-haired Belva became a bride.

Belva and Uriah moved into their own home on a small farm which was the gift of John McNall. Uriah worked the land. For eighteen months the couple were completely happy. Then one spring morning when Belva was feeding the chickens Uriah was brought home on a farm wagon, broken and bleeding from a sawmill accident.

The village doctor was pessimistic. For weeks Uriah hovered between life and death, then began to improve. He never became fully well, however, remaining a semi-invalid. Belva's father and her younger brother Warren took care of the farm.

Always Belva hoped that Uriah would regain his vigor. She was encouraged when her baby was born and color came back to Uriah's face and he did a little light work on the farm.

It was to be the height of his improvement. Thereafter Belva saw him become feebler and more tired, until even holding the baby Lura overtaxed his strength. Uriah died when Lura was three.

Soon occurred the incident which Belva cited when she asked why she had joined the fight for equal rights.

Her parents offered her and Lura a home. John McNall asked her to come live with him. She declined the offers. She preferred, she said, to stay on the farm and earn her own living. "Besides," she told her mother, "it is not enough for me to go to cornhuskings and sewing bees. I am terribly lonely without Uriah. I need something to do; I need to be occupied."

She decided to return to teaching. Dressed in widow's black, she went to the courthouse where the village trustees were meeting and applied for a regular teaching position in the district school.

She withdrew from the room for a few minutes while the men talked over her application, then was called back and told the job was hers.

Pleased, she thanked them. Then she said, "May I ask what my salary will be?"

The bearded chairman answered, "We have settled on that, Mrs. McNall. Your salary will be seven dollars each week."

Her face whitened. "Would you please tell me the salaries of the men teachers?"

The chairman said, "That would depend on their qualifications, but between ten and fifteen dollars a week."

"Would I have as many pupils as they?" Belva asked. "Would my hours be the same?"

Puzzled, the chairman nodded. Her mouth trembled from anger. "That is unfair," she said. "I cannot take the position." She turned and left.

The wife of the Methodist minister was her friend. When Uriah was alive she and the minister had often come to the farm to visit. After Uriah's death the minister's wife had consoled Belva, urged her to come to her if she needed help.

Leaving the courthouse, Belva walked swiftly past Mc-Nall's Corners to the little house where her friend lived. The woman welcomed her and gave her a glass of milk and some cookies.

Belva told her about the interview. "It is unjust," she said hotly. "There shouldn't be one standard for men teachers and another for women. You're my friend. Will you go to the trustees on my behalf? Make them understand that this is wrong."

The other woman shook her head. "Belva, my dear," she said, "I cannot help you. There is nothing either of us can do. This is the way of the world."

Belva left the minister's wife, still angry, discouraged, hearing again and again the words "It is the way of the world." Of course, she thought. It is true. The small salary set by the trustees was not intended as a slight to her, to Belva McNall. No. It was merely a tiny incident in society's conduct toward women.

All her life she had seen evidence of woman's inferior position. All a woman's possessions became her husband's when she married—she had known that. She had known that a woman could not bring suit under the law, no more than a child could. Where was the woman who had been admitted to a profession? Where? All the doctors, lawyers, ministers were men. How had the meanings of these things escaped her?

In the days that followed she thought: Surely I am not the only woman who is angry, who is questioning. There must be others. Who are they? What are they saying and doing?

She sent away for newspapers from the big cities, Boston and New York. She learned that as long as five years ago women demanding equal rights had held a convention at the home of Elizabeth Cady Stanton in Seneca Falls, New York. She learned that a militant equal rights organization had been formed. She read about Lucy Stone of Boston and a newcomer to the movement, Susan B. Anthony.

Belva felt a kinship with these women. They inspired her. How able they seemed, how courageous. How keen their arguments and ideas. How limited by comparison were her own ideas. If only she had had more education.

The story that Belva McNall had refused a teaching position because she would not be paid a man's salary had spread through the village, causing whispers and criticism. Her sister Rachel told her impatiently, "People are saying that you didn't act like a lady at the trustees meeting and I must say I agree with them."

Belva began to express her new ideas of equality and quote the women she had read about. The criticism became sharper. A few weeks after the trustees meeting she really gave Royalton something to talk about. She made up her mind to go to college.

When she mentioned it at home Rachel burst into tears. "What has gotten into you?" she cried. "Why do you have to be different? Everyone is talking about you. I'm afraid to think what they'll say now. You, a married woman with a child, going off to college. Why, you're twenty-four years old."

Belva's mother was more sympathetic. "My dear," she said to Belva, "I don't understand these notions of yours. But you're hurting no one. Do what your heart tells you. Go to college. I will be a mother to your little girl."

To get money for her education Belva sold her little farm. She applied for admission to Genesee College in the New York town of Lima and was accepted. In the fall of the year she took the stage to Lima and began her studies.

College was all that she had hoped for.

Classrooms and students quarters were housed in a new $20,000 building, a huge sum at the time. She went to classes and studied with a never-flagging eagerness. She took part in the student movement against slavery, attended debates on important political issues, and heard lectures on temperance.

Harriet Beecher Stowe's book *Uncle Tom's Cabin* was published and Belva read it over and over, crying with each reading.

Twice each week she wrote home, including a message to be read to Lura. Occasionally she sent her little girl a gift—a doll, a pair of pretty mittens, a picture book.

Returning home for the summer vacation, she cried with happiness when she saw how Lura had grown. She spent every possible hour with her child, reading to her, telling her stories of life at college, singing her to sleep. In the fall Belva returned to Genesee for her second and final year.

The months flew by. Suddenly it was June. Her marks in the final examinations were among the highest in the class and Dr. Joseph Cummings, President of Genesee, congratulated Belva on her thesis. She was graduated with honors.

On Dr. Cummings' recommendation she was offered the position of Preceptress of the Union School at Lockport, New York. Belva was flattered and pleased. This public high school with some 600 students was known throughout the Northeast for the excellence of its standards and program. The classrooms were large and cheerful. There was a well-equipped laboratory for teaching chemistry, and facilities for instruction in other sciences.

Belva wrote the Lockport school board that she was accepting the position.

Lockport in the 1850's was a prosperous transportation and manufacturing center. The construction of a series of locks which brought the Erie Canal through the Lockport gorge had made the town a relay point for settlers on their way to the Northwest and for bargeloads of manufactured goods and farm produce.

Flour mills sprang up, also a glass factory, a barrel plant, textile plants. In Lockport was brewed Dr. Merchant's Gargling Oil, a popular patent medicine claimed to be effective against more than one hundred diseases of humans and animals.

Belva made a life for herself and Lura. She rented two sunny rooms in a farmhouse just outside the town and she and Lura took their meals with the farmer and his wife. Lura went to school.

Belva directed the Union School and herself taught classes in higher mathematics, logic, rhetoric, and natural science. At the same time she tried constantly to incorporate into the school program her philosophy of equality of the sexes.

She urged her teachers to do as much to encourage scholarship among the girls as they did among the boys and not take the attitude that because most of the girls were "merely" going to be wives and mothers academic achievement was not important to them.

She introduced a course in public speaking for the girl pupils. It is offered in every high school now. But then it shocked many Lockport parents. Ladies, according to the view of the time, did not speak in public before audiences.

Mrs. McNall taught this course herself and it became popular among the girls. But the parents had hardly gotten used to it when the Preceptress took an even more radical step.

Pausing one day to observe the boys going through their gymnastic exercises, she thought: Girls should be doing this thing too. It is healthful, good for the body.

She returned to her office and wrote an announcement that henceforth gymnastic exercises would be held daily for the girls.

She appointed herself leader for the gymnastic exercises. At first the girls giggled and did the exercises hesitantly and abashedly. But they grew to like them and in a few weeks were imitating the Preceptress with assurance and vigor.

A number of parents protested and some demanded that Mrs. McNall be dismissed, but she had the support of a forward-looking school board and was able to continue.

In Lockport Belva served on committees of the woman's rights movement, and once she helped to arrange a meeting at which Susan Anthony spoke. Miss Anthony, herself a former schoolteacher, stayed at the farmhouse with Belva. The two women were instantly drawn to each other and for the two nights of Miss Anthony's visit stayed up almost until dawn talking.

Belva McNall remained in Lockport through the Civil War. She hated war and she prayed for peace, but a peace which would restore the unity of the nation and insure the freedom of the Negro. During the war she presided over the Lockport Ladies Aid Society and spent many hours sewing uniforms for the troops, knitting socks, and rolling bandages.

With the coming of peace much of her contentment with life in Lockport departed. The town now seemed to her small and the events which occurred there insignificant compared to the happenings in places like New York, Boston, and Washington. She decided to visit the nation's capital, which attracted her particularly, and settle there if she found she liked it.

She and Lura, now in her early teens, spent a few days visiting in Royalton and then traveled to Washington by rail.

They admired the sandstone and marble Capitol building and the White House, watched Congress at work and viewed the foreign embassies. Mother and daughter agreed that they wanted to stay on.

Belva easily found a job teaching at a seminary for young ladies, in which Lura was enrolled as a pupil. A year and a half later Belva founded her own seminary.

The new school did well. More important, love of a man and his love for her came into Belva's life again.

Troubled by an aching tooth, Belva asked newly made friends to recommend a dentist. They sent her to Dr. Ezekiel Lockwood. She came home from the visit smiling happily.

"Why, Mother," Lura exclaimed, "have you been to the dentist or the theater?"

"I'm happy because it's so good to be free of pain again," Belva said. "And that Dr. Lockwood is such a charming man. He's handsome. He's tall and lean and somehow he reminds me of your father. There's something about the way he wrinkles his forehead when he's thinking. And he agrees with me that it's shameful that women are not permitted to vote."

Lura said mischievously, "Don't let him get away, Mother. Any man who has all those qualities is a prize indeed."

"Oh, Lura," Belva said, "I only met Dr. Lockwood for the first time today. And he is much older than I." She smiled. "I told him he could call on me tomorrow night."

Dr. Lockwood and Belva McNall were married in late winter of 1868 with Lura their only attendant.

The Lockwood family, Dr. Lockwood, Belva and Lura, settled in an apartment on F Street. No longer needing to earn a living, Belva gave up her school. Within a year of her marriage she gave birth to a girl, named Jessie Belva.

If Belva had a regret it was that the day was not long enough for all the things she wanted to do. She cooked and kept house, cared for her baby, led an active social life and worked hard for the equal rights movement.

She and Dr. Lockwood organized a chapter of the equal rights organization in Washington. Its meetings, at which Belva presided, were held in the parlor of her home. It was slow, discouraging work trying to build the chapter.

Sometimes twenty people, men and women, Negro and white, came to the meetings; other times there were as few as three or four. The meetings were announced in the Washington papers and on some occasions rowdies came and jeered and heckled the speakers.

Meanwhile, Belva Lockwood was working on an equal rights reform project to which she was especially drawn because of her experience with the Royalton trustees over salary. Several thousand women were employed in the federal civil service, the majority in Washington. Some held positions of greater responsibility than the men with whom they worked. But the most the women could be paid was seventy-five dollars a month.

Shortly after her marriage, Mrs. Lockwood began collecting signatures to a petition to Congress for a bill providing that women employees be paid according to merit, like men.

Going about this work, she felt handicapped. Men whom she tried to convince had a much greater familiarity with law and government regulations than she. Though she was convinced she was right, she was often defeated or felt frustrated in argument.

Several Congressmen to whom she spoke were interested in her effort. They asked her to prepare a bill. She tried but the language of the law seemed to her like a foreign tongue. She had to go to an attorney for help.

The whole thing irked her. Why were women ignorant of such matters? Here in Washington one could locate lawyers everywhere, but all men. If only one of these lawyers were a woman, and if she were sympathetic to equal rights, how valuable she would be. What an inspiration to other women.

Thinking this, she struck her forehead with the palm of her hand. "Belva Ann Lockwood," she said, "you are a dunderhead. Why don't you study law?"

A few days later she said to Dr. Lockwood and Lura at

dinner, "I have something to tell you . . ." She fell silent while they looked at her expectantly.

She said, "Don't laugh at me. I don't care if you get angry or think I'm being foolish, but please don't laugh."

Lura held up her right hand; Dr. Lockwood did the same. "We promise," Lura said.

Belva rattled it out quickly. "I'm going to study law. I'm going to prepare myself to be a lawyer. I want to practice before the bar." She held herself tight, waiting for their reaction. When they spoke the tears of gladness came into her eyes.

Lura exclaimed, "Mother, how wonderful." Dr. Lockwood stood up and embraced her. "My Belva, I'm very proud to be your husband," he said.

She sent letters to several nearby law schools asking to be admitted as a student. In the course of several weeks the replies came in, all essentially the same: it was not the policy of the school to admit women, or, the faculty was opposed to the admission of women.

She also visited the National University Law School in Washington, which had recently been established. There she spoke to the vice-chancellor, whom she knew slightly. He was sympathetic to equal rights.

The vice-chancellor, whose name was Wedgewood, said he himself approved of what Mrs. Lockwood was trying to do but he was virtually certain that the faculty would refuse to accept her. However, he said he would submit her application to the faculty and do everything he could to persuade its members to approve it.

Several weeks later Belva was called by Mr. Wedgewood to his office. "I have done everything I could," he told her.

"The faculty has discussed your application at three meetings but I couldn't win over even one man. The faculty's answer is 'no.'"

She had anticipated this and was prepared with another resource. "Mr. Wedgewood," she said, "will you give me private lessons in the law?" He started, then sat musing, tapping his nose with a pencil. "Yes, Mrs. Lockwood, I will," he said. "I will do it."

He stood up. But she remained seated. She had something further to ask for her cause. "Mr. Wedgewood," she said with a smile, "it's as easy to teach a dozen as one. Won't you conduct a private class for women? I am sure there are a number of women in Washington who would be grateful for the opportunity."

The vice-chancellor swallowed. He said, "A class—" He shook his head in admiration of her. "I will," he said. "I will. And now, Mrs. Lockwood, please go home before I commit myself to anything further."

For some months Lura had been keeping company with a young pharmacist named De Forest Ormes, and shortly before Belva began her law studies the couple were married. They made their home with Dr. and Mrs. Lockwood, and Lura took over much of the housekeeping duties and the care of the baby while Belva went daily to class in Mr. Wedgewood's office.

Belva Lockwood was forty years old when she heard her first lectures on Coke and Blackstone in 1870, one of a handful of women struggling against the historic exclusion of their sex from the law.

In Philadelphia Caroline Burnham was then applying to the legal department of the University of Pennsylvania and being told by Spencer Miller, the dean of the faculty, that if women or Negroes were admitted he would resign. However, she was later admitted as a student and completed the course. But it was not until 1883 that she was admitted to the bar in the conclusion of a bitter fight.

In 1870 Arabella A. Mansfield, who had "read" law in a private legal office, already was a veteran of a year before the bar of Iowa. At the same time Ada Kepley, said to be the first woman to be graduated from a law school, was getting her diploma from Union College in Chicago.

Meanwhile the Illinois bar was refusing to admit Mrs. Myra Bradwell of Chicago on the grounds that (1) as a married woman her contracts would not be binding, (2) the admission of females was prohibited under common law, (3) to admit a woman to the bar would imply that women were eligible to be judges and even governors of states, (4) to admit a female lawyer would endanger the "delicacy" of the female sex.

Mrs. Bradwell carried an appeal to the Supreme Court but this body upheld the ruling of the Illinois court.

Fifteen women enrolled in the private law course conducted by Mr. Wedgewood, but only two saw it through to the end in 1873, Mrs. Lockwood and a Mrs. Lydia Hall.

During the time that Mrs. Lockwood was attending school she was also working for equal rights.

She wrote a bill providing that "all clerks and employees in Civil Service of the United States shall be paid irrespective of sex with reference to the character and amount of services performed by them."

S. M. Arnell, member of the House of Representatives from Tennessee, introduced the bill for her. Members of the equal rights movement in a dozen states collected signatures to a petition urging the bill's adoption while in Washington Mrs. Lockwood went about talking to Congressmen.

The bill was passed—an important victory in the rise of American women toward equality. One of its side results was that it helped establish Mrs. Lockwood as an important figure in the equal rights struggle.

During her law school years Belva lost a loved one for the second time. Returning from school one afternoon, she was met at the door by Lura, who told her worriedly that the baby was ill. Jessie was crying as though in pain, her skin was hot and dry. "Her nose has been bleeding," Lura said.

Belva clutched at the post of the child's bed for support. It sounded like typhoid, which took scores of lives in Washington each year. Lura ran for the doctor, but he was helpless against the disease.

Belva stayed with her child day and night, nursing her, praying for her life, but Jessie died.

For weeks Belva did not leave her home, but wept and mourned her pretty little girl, feeling that life was empty and purposeless. Dr. Lockwood, who seemed to have aged by ten years after the death of his child, and Lura and her husband consoled Belva and supported her with their love.

Then, to forget the pain of her loss, Belva forced herself to return to her studies and work. But for months, whenever she saw a child who reminded her of Jessie, she felt a stab in her heart.

Mr. Wedgewood asked Mrs. Lockwood and Mrs. Hall to come to see him. They chatted for a few moments about the weather, unusually warm for May, then he said, "I have two items of news for you ladies, one good, one bad. The good is that both of you have passed the final examinations. And with excellent marks. The bad is that the faculty refuses to approve diplomas for you. I pointed out that you have met every qualification, but the faculty says that the school's standards would be lowered if it granted degrees to women.

"There are no means by which the faculty can be compelled," Mr. Wedgewood added, "because after all you ladies were not regularly enrolled students."

Mrs. Lockwood stopped biting on the edge of a fingernail. "Would it do any good if I called on President Grant?" she asked. "He is the titular head of the school and when Miss Anthony spoke with him recently he seemed friendly to women's rights."

"N-no," Mr. Wedgewood said. "I agree that President Grant is friendly, but I don't think you could get to see him on a personal matter. Also I don't think he would want to upset the rules of the faculty. However, you have given me an idea, Mrs. Lockwood."

"What do you propose to do?" Mrs. Lockwood asked.

The vice-chancellor shook his head. "I don't want to arouse your hopes. It may not work. Just be patient for a few weeks."

Mr. Wedgewood subsequently sent to the President of the United States the diplomas of the graduating class of the National University Law School to be signed. Among them were two made out in the names of Mrs. Lockwood and Mrs. Hall.

The diplomas came back from the White House. All had been signed.

What happened in the White House? Did the former

commander of the Union armies notice that two of the names were of women? Or did the President, busy with conferences and problems of government, sign the diplomas without reading them along with scores of other documents presented daily for signing by his secretaries? No one knows the answers.

Within a month, Mrs. Lockwood's diploma in hand, Mr. Wedgewood went before the bar of the District of Columbia and moved that she be admitted to practice. Possibly the officers of the bar were influenced by Mr. Wedgewood or they may have been sympathetic to Mrs. Lockwood. In any case, they gave their approval.

Mrs. Lockwood was a lawyer.

From the very beginning, Mrs. Lockwood was a success as a lawyer even though she was a woman. People in trouble liked the slender woman with the strong face and were assured by her calm confidence. Moreover, she knew her law and in the courtroom she spoke with an earnest effectiveness.

At first most of her clients were women: women seeking divorces, women deserted by their husbands, women charged with crimes. As her reputation grew, men also came to her office in her home on F Street with a variety of legal problems.

She never turned down a case because a would-be client was without money. As she became known for this, she was asked to try many claims against the government by people who could not pay her a fee unless she was successful in court. Many of her clients in this category were Indians, to whom she was quite sympathetic.

In one claims case, which was reported in newspapers throughout the country, she won an award of fifty thousand dollars in bounties for sailors of the United States Navy.

In 1875, when she had been practicing law for two years, Belva Lockwood applied to the United States Supreme Court for the right to practice before it. Because she was a woman, the nation's highest court refused even to consider the application.

She became convinced that the Supreme Court would never of its own accord admit a woman lawyer. She resolved to try to obtain passage of a bill in Congress which would open the Supreme Court to women attorneys. She wrote a bill and went about talking to Congressmen.

Meanwhile, seeking in other ways to widen the opportunities for women attorneys, she applied for admission to the bar of Maryland. Judge Magruder of the court at Upper Marlboro set a date for announcement of his decision. Mrs. Lockwood and a group of friends went to the court to hear it.

Before Judge Magruder finished uttering his first sentence Mrs. Lockwood knew what the decision would be.

"In the statutes of the state of Maryland," he said coldly, "there is no reference to feminine pronouns. Searching the statutes, I have found only he, him, and his—never she, her, or hers.

"Women are not needed in the courts. Women are not wanted in the courts. The place for women is in the home, waiting upon their husbands, bringing up their children, making beds and dusting furniture. . . .

"This application is denied."

Angered, she was on her feet. "Your Honor," she said, "I request permission to reply to your statement."

"No," the judge said. "There is too much business before this court."

She persisted. "Will you spare me a few moments during the noon recess?"

Judge Magruder thought. "Very well," he said. "During the noon recess—a few moments."

He did not keep his word. At noon the judge had the courtroom cleared and the doors locked and he went home for lunch.

"I'm going to speak," Mrs. Lockwood told her friends. "I'm so angry I'll burst if I don't speak."

"But how?" one woman asked. "To whom?"

"You'll see," Belva answered. "Come with me."

She stepped up to the courthouse veranda and gripped the rail. "Sir," she said to a male passerby, "I want to tell you about an act of injustice just perpetrated in this courtroom." He paused and she spoke to him. Another man stopped out of curiosity and waited to listen, then another, and more until she had an audience of two dozen.

She told of Judge Magruder's decision and quoted his reasons for making it. "I have been married twice," she said. "I am a wife and mother. And I became a lawyer, but never have I neglected my duties to my husband and my children.

"I am not asking any special privilege, merely the same opportunity to utilize my training and experience which is available to any man."

She declared that many women had to work to support themselves and their children. "If the professions are to be closed to them," she said, "they must work as servants, factory hands, or clerks regardless of their intelligence and ability. Thousands of women in the North and South have been made widows by the recent war. What is to become of them if they are not permitted to earn a decent livelihood?"

One man shouted, "I'll take two or three of the prettier ones." The men guffawed and slapped each other on the back. But they appreciated that she laughed too and they gave her their attention again.

She fought on and was admitted to practice in Maryland. Later she also opened the courts of Virginia to women lawyers by being admitted to practice in that state.

For the cause of women, and human betterment generally, she was active on many fronts. She was instrumental in obtaining the appointment of a matron to care for the women prisoners in the jail of Washington, D.C. It was said to be the first appointment of its kind in the country.

She induced the Washington authorities to provide special retiring parlors for women witnesses and their lawyers in the courthouses.

But her crowning achievement was her own admission— as the first woman attorney—to practice before the United States Supreme Court.

Three times she had a bill introduced in the House of Representatives to permit women attorneys to practice before the Supreme Court and each time it was defeated. In 1878, on her fourth attempt, the bill passed the House with 169 votes in favor and 87 against.

But in the Senate the bill died.

The next year Mrs. Lockwood had the bill introduced into the House again. It passed. And this time it passed the Senate too. Senators speaking in its favor used material which Mrs. Lockwood had prepared. The bill was signed into law by President Rutherford B. Hayes.

On March 3, 1879, Mrs. Belva Ann Lockwood was admitted to the bar of the United States Supreme Court.

Lovely in brown silk, her hair curled on her forehead and drawn into a knot at the nape of her neck, she took the official oath before a distinguished audience of government leaders. Accepting the parchment certificate of her membership, she prayed silently, "Please, God, make me worthy of this high trust."

The next year the woman who was the first of her sex to practice before the Supreme Court took part in establishing another historic precedent involving that body. She moved before the court that Samuel Lowry of Alabama be admitted to practice. The court approved, thus admitting the first Negro attorney to practice before it.

In her long legal career Mrs. Lockwood argued a number of cases before the Supreme Court. In the best-known of these, she represented a body of thousands of Cherokee Indians demanding payment for land which they had given up on the promise that they would be compensated.

The Supreme Court upheld the claims of the Indians, and the government paid them nearly three-quarters of a million dollars.

On her fiftieth birthday it occurred to Belva Lockwood that the years were going by more swiftly. Her hair was touched with gray, but that, she thought, befitted a grandmother. Lura had two children, both girls, and soon was to give birth to a boy.

How happy Ezekiel would have been, she thought. But Dr. Lockwood had died in his sleep in 1877, nine years after his marriage to Belva.

From many states came letters to her from women and girls asking advice on a law career and how to deal with their personal difficulties which seemed to prevent it. Despite heavy demands on her time, Belva Lockwood replied to them all.

She corresponded with other women lawyers to form an association. The members called it the Equity Club and in letters they addressed each other as "Dear Sister in Law."

Mrs. Lockwood took great satisfaction in the growing number of women practicing law. In 1882 she knew of fifty-six in the United States, thirty-one of them graduates of law schools. By the end of the century she was able to count 1,010 women in practice.

It is impossible to calculate how many were inspired to study law and were sustained in time of difficulty by the example and the advice of the country's leading woman lawyer.

But Belva Lockwood was never satisfied with what had been achieved. For women she wanted every opportunity, every right, every privilege, every office open to men—even the Presidency of the United States. In 1884 she became the first woman in history to run for the Presidency.

She did not seek a nomination. It came to her when she wrote a wrathful letter.

Every four years the equal rights organization sent representatives to the national conventions of the major political parties to urge that they include in their platforms an equal rights plank.

In 1884 the representatives to the Republican National Convention in Chicago were Mrs. Lockwood and her friends Phoebe Couzins.

Mrs. Lockwood was given a few minutes to address the resolutions committee. "For all the good I did," she later told friends, "I might as well have been speaking in my own parlor. When I finished pleading for an equal rights plank the resolutions committee quickly voted to refer the matter to a subcommittee. And that was the end of it."

The treatment given Frances E. Willard, a noted educator, woman's rights leader and spokesman for temperance, in the resolutions committee meeting disgusted Mrs. Lockwood.

Miss Willard came before the committee to advocate that the party adopt a temperance plank. She presented a petition signed by 20,000 persons, the work of many months.

"Representatives of the distilling industry were permitted to be present when Miss Willard stated her case," Belva said. "They jeered her, insulted her. One man seized the petitions and threw them on the floor."

Mrs. Lockwood and Phoebe Couzins returned to Washington angry and bitter. Mrs. Lockwood took up the legal work which had accumulated during her absence. A few weeks later she received in the mail a circular signed by her friends Susan B. Anthony and Elizabeth Stanton urging the women of the nation to support the Republican candidate James G. Blaine.

It was the belief of Miss Anthony and Mrs. Stanton that even though the Republican Party had not adopted an equal rights plank it numbered among its leaders more supporters of the woman's cause than the Democrats. The two women maintained that it was good long-run strategy to support Blaine.

Belva gazed at the circular in stunned disbelief. She thought: How can Susan and Elizabeth do this in the face of the Republican refusal to take up their cause? Of course, the Democrats were no better. The equal rights movement should endorse neither party. Oh, if women could only vote. If only—she threw up her head. An idea had just come to her.

"Lillie," she said to her stenographer, "I'm going to write a letter. Please type it and send it to Mrs. Marietta Stow, editor of the *Woman's Herald of Industry*, in San Francisco." She grinned, "I wish there was such a thing as fire-proof paper because it's going to be a sizzling letter." This was her letter to her editor friend Mrs. Stow:

"If women in the United States are not permitted to vote, there is no law against their being voted for, and if elected, filling the highest office in the gift of the people.

"Why not nominate women for important places? Is not Victoria Empress of India? Is not history full of precedent of women rulers? Have we not among our own country-women persons of as much talent and ability?

"The Republican Party, claiming to be the party of progress, has little but insult for women when they appear before its conventions. It is time we had our own party, our own platform, and our own nominees.

"We shall never have equal rights until we take them, nor respect until we command it. If we act up to our convictions of justice and equal rights, we will not go far wrong."

The letter was published in Mrs. Stow's newspaper, a periodical devoted to advancing the cause of women. Subsequent issues carried other letters commenting on it, some approving, some criticizing.

On a mid-September day Belva was home with a cold. Lura brought the mail to her and then went to the kitchen to heat some soup. Some minutes went by. Lura heard her mother cry out, "Heavens! Heavens! Lura, come quickly."

Lura ran to her mother in the parlor. Belva was blushing. She was holding an open letter in her hand. "Lura," she said weakly, "I have been nominated for the Presidency by the Equal Rights Party of the Pacific Coast."

For three days Belva carried the letter around with her, not showing it to anyone, but thinking about it. She made up her mind to accept the nomination and she so wrote the party at its San Francisco headquarters. Mrs. Stow, nominated for the vice-presidency, also accepted.

Belva Lockwood took over the leadership of the campaign. Mrs. Stow's newspaper was converted into a campaign organ. Although the equal rights movement officially took no position on the new Equal Rights Party, and Miss Anthony and Mrs. Stanton and a number of its leaders were opposed to it, party organizations were established in ten states.

State conventions were organized. Because no one votes in the District of Columbia, Belva herself organized a convention in Maryland. At this meeting, held on a farm in Prince George County, she made her formal acceptance speech before some sixty men and women, including nine reporters from Washington and Baltimore newspapers.

"Rise up and take your place in government," she urged the women of the nation . . . In December this campaign of our Equal Rights Party will pass into history and become the entering wedge—the first practical movement in the struggle for equal rights. Although we may not see the end of our struggle for some time, this is the beginning of that end."

The Equal Rights Party managed to established an electoral ticket in six states.

During the campaign Mrs. Lockwood spoke almost

nightly and gave dozens of newspaper interviews. Before Election Day nearly everyone who read a newspaper had heard of the "lady candidate."

The campaign had an amusing sidelight. In a number of cities young men organized themselves into so-called Mother Hubbard Clubs and Broom Brigades. Dressed in women's clothing and carrying brooms or mops and pails, they paraded, shouting mocking slogans urging "elect a lady to the White House."

Some of her supporters were indignant, but Belva found the young men funny. "They don't intend any harm," she said, "and they have inspired many political cartoons."

Grover Cleveland, the Democratic nominee, was elected President. In the official results Mrs. Lockwood got 379 votes in New Hampshire, 1,336 votes in New York, 374 in Michigan, 1,008 in Illinois, 318 in Maryland, and 734 in California.

All these votes necessarily were cast by men only.

The Equal Rights Party claimed that it received hundreds and perhaps thousands of votes more in other states which were not counted.

Mrs. Lockwood was satisfied with the result of the campaign. "Its major accomplishment," she said, "is that it brought to the attention of the people of the country the issue of equal rights more vigorously than ever before."

Four years later she was again a candidate for the Presidency on the ticket of the Equal Rights Party.

Anticipating the League of Nations and the United Nations, she drew up and had introduced in Congress in 1885 the first bill advocating an international court to keep the world peace.

The same year the State Department sent her to Switzerland as an American delegate to the Congress of Charities. It was the first of many missions she was to carry out for the American government; most of them were concerned with peace and international arbitration.

In 1890 she read a paper on disarmament at the International Peace Congress in London. After the Congress she wrote Lura:

"Everything went off very well. As long as you and the children and Forest are all well and happy I think I shall stay in England a while and take a series of courses at Oxford University. There is so much I don't know about so many things."

At eighty-four, with Europe on the verge of World War One, she made her last trip abroad as a representative of the State Department, carrying a peace message to the women of the world.

She gave her last message to the women of America during the Presidential campaign of 1916, speaking in behalf of the re-election of President Woodrow Wilson. Thus Mrs. Lockwood helped to return to office the President during whose term, and with whose support, the Equal Rights Amendment giving women the vote was adopted.

She died on May 19, 1917, at the age of 86 and was mourned by people of good will throughout the world.

Antoinette Brown

ANTOINETTE BROWN was twenty-one years old when she first told someone about her dream.

She was standing at the rail on the roof of an Erie Canal packet boat on her second night away from home, looking at the stars and breathing the fresh smell of the woods. A male voice said, "Good evening, my daughter." She turned and smiled a welcome at an elderly minister whom she had observed earlier among the passengers.

The minister and the girl remarked on the beauty of the night. Nettie asked him where his church was. "Here on the canal," the minister replied and explained that he was a missionary, saving souls among the captains and crews of the packets. "There is much wickedness on the canal," he said.

Every step of the horses on the towpath was bringing her closer to Oberlin Collegiate Institute in Ohio where she hoped to prepare herself to live her dream. Her heart was light. The minister seemed kindly, like a father. She spoke freely.

"I think God takes care of everyone," she said. "I believe

in that sort of God, a kind and gentle God, more like our
earthly fathers. Ever since I was a little girl I have wanted,
wanted so much, to talk to people about the kind of God I
believe in. So they won't fear a cruel and avenging monarch
who is often their God. So they won't be so afraid to live,
so afraid to die."

She hesitated a moment, but his nodding approval
prompted her to confide in him. She went on, "I have
never told anyone before. I have never told even my mother
or father. You see, sir, I hope one day to become a minister
of the gospel."

The missionary drew back a step. His face had turned
harsh. "You speak blasphemy, my daughter," he said. "Have
you not read what St. Paul wrote in his first letter to the
Corinthians? He said, 'Let your women keep silence in the
churches: for it is not permitted them to speak.'"

She said pleadingly, "Just because I am a woman can I
not do the Lord's work, comforting and succoring my
fellow men and women?"

Impatiently the minister answered, "Have you not read
the words of the blessed saint when he wrote to Timothy,
'I suffer not a woman to teach nor to usurp authority over
the man, but to be in silence.' Remember, to be in silence!"

She quivered, then quietly turned and went below to the
women's cabin.

It was her first taste of what she was to experience in her
striving to become a minister. She never forgot that night in
August of 1846.

Antoinette Louisa Brown lived a long time but even when
she was a very old lady her memory never failed her. She

could remember the log farmhouse in Henrietta in western New York where she was born in 1825. She could remember the names of Indians who lived in the forest close by.

She used to recall that she was little more than a baby when her father felt she was ready for school. A few days before her third birthday she began attending a little country school. "I sat in my teacher's lap to recite my lessons," she would say.

Nettie was one of ten children of Joseph and Abby Brown, four of whom died before she outgrew her teens.

Her father, a stoutish man, calm and slow speaking, was a farmer and justice of the peace. His neighbors, who respected his wisdom, called him Squire.

Nettie remembered her father as a gentle and tender man "who couldn't bear to hurt anyone." His mind was open to new ideas and he was sympathetic to reform. He had a higher regard for the abilities of women than was usual among men of his time.

The Squire was a man of great piety. When Nettie was a little girl he told her that in his youth he had wanted to become a minister but instead had to take over the operation of the family farm when his father was disabled fighting against the British in the War of Independence. Often Nettie heard her father say, "The service of God is man's noblest calling." Antoinette's older brother William made the Squire very happy by going off to college to prepare for the ministry.

Squire Brown read a great deal—antislavery pamphlets, newspaper accounts of debates in Congress, the plays of Shakespeare, the Bible, religious tracts of his Congregational Church. His fondness for reading and his duties as justice of the peace often kept him from overseeing the work on his farm. Mrs. Brown—tall, spare, energetic—managed capably in his place. The farm prospered. During Nettie's childhood, two small adjoining farms were purchased by the Squire and the log house was replaced by a larger one of stone.

Nettie used to say of her mother, "She was a woman of much executive ability. Always when she took hold of a task she saw it through."

Antoinette inherited her mother's determination. She had her father's calmness and gentleness.

Nettie was about five or six, she remembered, when her dream began—at first merely a mood, a pleasing emotion tinged with a little sadness. Each day the family gathered for prayer. The Squire's mother, who lived with them, took part, as did the maid and the hired man. The Squire read from the Bible in his slow thoughtful way; the group sang a hymn.

Nettie listened raptly. It seemed to her that when the Squire read from the Bible, God came into the room, a God who was kind, a God who loved all His children. She felt a sweetness and comfort. Here around her were those she loved most and who loved her, and here was God, blessing them in their love and unity.

She felt a yearning to bring others into this peaceful company. She thought of a peddler with tired eyes who had sold her mother an iron pot, a sick schoolmate, a neighboring farmer who the grown-ups said was destroying himself with whiskey.

At the end of each service she ran to her father, flung her arms around him and kissed him.

Usually her grandmother, who was in her eighties, prepared Nettie for bed, and when she was tucked in the old lady told her stories from the Bible and recited religious poems which she had learned as a child. Nettie's memory held fast the words of religion and she was fond of saying them aloud. They sounded good, godly.

It was a time when there was little literature for children and most of what there was had a religious character.

She was a happy, healthy child, enjoying school and farm life. Each spring there was a sugar festival when the maples were tapped and the sap was boiled down to syrup or sugar. This was followed by a possum hunt to rid the land of the little animals which destroyed the crops. In late summer the farmers gathered for the wheat harvest, and Nettie carried to the harvesters water spiced with vinegar and molasses.

In wintertime she and the other children of the community played on the ice of a pond near the Henrietta schoolhouse. The boys skated, but nothing so unfeminine was permitted girls. They slid or were pulled on sleds by the boys.

Nettie had a doll, like other little girls. Like other children, she often pretended; the doll became a baby. But the game she came to love the most in her childhood was a unique one. She interested several other girls in "playing church" in the Brown barn. The dark-haired Antoinette was the minister and the others made up the congregation.

This was an unusual idea, because Nettie had never known or even heard of a woman minister; for a woman had never been regularly ordained to the ministry.

Her dream was developing.

She was an intelligent child, and when she was nine she

was accepted into membership of the Congregational Church of her parents. Soon she was even speaking at meetings, telling how she loved God and felt uplifted by Him. Once her words so moved an elderly deacon that he exclaimed, "Out of the mouths of babes and sucklings the Lord hath perfected His praise!"

In bed Sunday night she would review the day-long church services, whispering one of the minister's phrases which had touched her. Sometimes she would fall asleep picturing herself as the minister.

She outgrew childhood's uninhibited pretense, and playing church was left in the past. But her dream remained, turning into a conscious longing to be a minister. She dreamed of a little church, of telling people about a gentle God of peace and love.

She dreamed in silence, though. She never spoke of her dream, nor for a time did she expect anything to come of it.

Nettie spent three years at Monroe Academy in Henrietta and at fifteen she began to teach in the little country schools nearby, boarding in the homes of farmers. Every Friday, when weather permitted, one of her sisters came for her on horseback so Nettie could spend the weekend at home.

Young men came calling on her. She was a pretty girl, quick to smile and warm. Moreover, she was well trained in the many skills required of a wife and mother in a time when nearly everything a farm family needed had to be made in the home, and was usually made by the woman.

She was happy when the young men came. Soon there was one she showed special affection for, a young towheaded farmer with a shy grin. They fell in love and he proposed marriage. She wanted a husband, a home, children, but she couldn't bring herself to say yes. Something she couldn't yet define seemed to prevent it.

The young man's visits became more infrequent, then ceased. Later Nettie heard of his marriage to a girl in another village and for a few weeks she was unhappy.

A year passed. As she grew in age and wisdom, a decision to try to become a minister was building up imperceptibly in her mind. It was this which had kept her from marrying, for as a wife she would be expected to bear children, do endless chores—studies, a career would be impossible. The decision thrust itself into her consciousness. She was determined to try to become a minister.

Nettie didn't tell her parents. For now she wanted to spare them the fear she knew they would feel for a daughter challenging the powerful taboos of society and religion. However, she began to think of her further education in preparation for the ministry.

Her attention was drawn to Oberlin Collegiate Institute, founded a few years before by two missionaries in the wilderness of Ohio's Western Reserve. Oberlin admitted Negroes and women. Better yet, it conducted a theological school for properly qualified students. Nettie set Oberlin as her first goal.

She went to her father and asked him to help her with funds to attend Oberlin. The Squire replied that he was sorry, but he couldn't help her. It would take every dollar he could spare to send his sons to college and he didn't think it would be right to sacrifice the education of a boy for that of a girl. A boy, he explained kindly, would have much more use for a higher education.

Antoinette resolved to go to college even if her father could not help her. She would continue teaching and save every possible penny until she had enough funds to make at least a beginning at Oberlin.

It took her three years to accumulate the money. Then she applied to Oberlin, describing the extent of her schooling, and was accepted as a junior in the Ladies' Literary Course. After two years' study she could apply for admission to the theological school.

On a summer day of 1846, Antoinette Brown left Henrietta for the ten-day journey to Ohio and Oberlin.

Oberlin Collegiate Institute. Physically it was primitive. Seven plain wooden buildings on a stump-dotted campus three hours by stage from Cleveland. Oberlin was poor and struggling, but it was imbued with a living philosophy of progress lacking in many of the older colleges in the East.

The sons of slaves and the sons of white bankers attended class together. Here coeducation was undertaken for the first time in an American college. Most of the five hundred students were actively concerned with the great social problems of the nation—slavery, drink, prostitution, wages, and working conditions. The mood of Oberlin was one of piety and earnestness.

Antoinette loved it. And though she experienced rebuffs and denials, and struggled and was hurt, she never stopped loving it. She studied hard, in class and in her tiny board-walled room on the third floor of Ladies' Hall. She attended discussions and debates. She made friends and to two of them she confided her ambition.

One was Lucy Stone, a pretty, young woman from Brookfield, Massachusetts, who vowed she would dedicate her life to working for reform and woman's rights.

Nettie liked Lucy right away and their affection grew although they disagreed constantly. Lucy wanted immediate freedom for the slaves no matter what the consequences were to the nation. Nettie, too, detested slavery but favored a gradual approach to its elimination. Lucy declared that a woman who wanted a career should never marry. Nettie said she would like to marry after she had been ordained. Nettie criticized Lucy for dressing too plainly. Lucy chided Nettie when she wore a dress with frills or put a rose in her hair.

James Tefft, a gaunt westerner who planned to enter the theological school and later serve as a missionary, became Nettie's other good friend. One day he overtook her walking on the campus and introduced himself. Nettie blushed because she knew he had been staring at her in the student dining hall and she wanted to meet him.

"Please, Miss Brown, may I call on you?" he asked. She considered his request, thinking that he looked friendly and his gray eyes were kind, but he didn't wait for a reply. "Capital!" he said. "I'll be there tonight at seven," and walked off with long strides.

She wore her prettiest dress that evening and as they walked under the stars he told her that her eyes were the color of the morning sky and that she looked beautiful.

They went on many more walks together. They read poetry, attended lectures and concerts, and long before he spoke the words she knew that he loved her. Her love for him grew more slowly.

At the end of her first year at Oberlin Nettie went to Rochester, Michigan, to teach in a private school and add to her dwindling funds. Lucy and James took her to the railroad station. James kissed her before she boarded the train.

Nettie was an outstanding student in her senior year, but its closing weeks brought increasing anxiety. Soon she would apply for admission to the theological school and she feared the response.

Her goal required a greater liberality toward women than even Oberlin was practicing. Oberlin still refused to permit its women students to speak on a public platform, and a professor who had arranged a debate between Lucy and Nettie was reprimanded and threatened with expulsion. Even coeducation did not have the full support of the faculty. Some professors privately opposed it by refusing to call on women students, by criticizing them more sharply than the men and grading them more severely.

She spent a Saturday writing two letters. One was her application to the faculty of the theological school. The other went to her parents. She told Squire and Mrs. Brown that she was trying to enter the theological school. For years, she wrote, she had cherished the dream of serving God and mankind in the pulpit. She added that she prayed that they would understand and approve. She closed by writing that the money she had earned teaching was almost entirely spent and she hoped that her father could now help her financially.

The reaction of the faculty came first—disbelief and anger. They took up her application at a special meeting and member after member denounced her as "reckless," "blasphemous," and "defiant of Christian precepts." Two professors said more calmly that they, too, were opposed to admitting a woman, but didn't the Oberlin charter state that the college facilities must be open to everyone, regardless of race, color, or sex?

The meeting ended in an impasse. The faculty did not want to admit her but could find no grounds for refusing. They referred the problem to the board of trustees.

Both groups tabled the matter while they sent spokesmen to reason with Antoinette. They came to her singly and in groups. Didn't she know, they asked, that even if she were permitted to study theology no church in the land would call her—a woman—to its pulpit? She would just be wasting years in study without purpose while subjecting Oberlin to ridicule and censure. They quoted St. Paul to her. Did she intend to defy the teachings of the Bible?

She told them all, "I will not change my mind. I am not defying the Bible. I believe that the writings of St. Paul are being misinterpreted, and one day I am going to try to prove it."

The men, having failed to dissuade her, sent their wives. The women invited Nettie to their homes for tea and each said much the same thing. They urged her to think of marriage, a home, children. She would make a fine wife for a minister. However, if she wanted a career, why not teach? There was such a great need in America for teachers.

Nettie listened day after day. The tension and anger grew in her. But to all who sought to influence her she replied calmly and politely. After each talk she fled to her room and prayed for forgiveness of her anger.

Caught between Nettie's determination and the pledges of the college charter, the faculty and trustees convened in a joint session and devised a compromise. She would be permitted to attend classes in the theological school, but she would not be a registered student.

Nettie received the news with elation. She was going to be permitted to study theology! The limitation imposed by the authorities did not then seem to her important. For four days her eyes shone with happiness and James whispered to her, "You're becoming more beautiful every time I see you." And then a blow came from home.

She opened the letter from her father and read, "I am shocked by your audacity and lack of wisdom. I cannot believe this thing. Your mother is prostrate. I will not aid you . . . I am doing you a kindness in refusing to help you carry out a plan which can bring you only unhappiness and disgrace."

She felt as if her father had beaten her. Better if he had. No physical punishment could cause the pain she now felt. She had hoped that he would approve of her dream, at least understand how much it meant to her. A father understands and sympathizes with a son. Why should it be different with a daughter? Why?

Again and again she read the letter, seeking a word of comfort but finding none. And how could she continue in school? Her money was spent. Had she fought this far only to have to retreat?

She went about her school work ill and depressed. Lucy and James, to whom she showed the letter from home, tried to console her. She begged them to leave her alone. After class each day she went to her room and lay on her bed for hours, staring at the ceiling in anger and despair.

And then her courage and healthy personality began to assert themselves. An awareness of her strength and capability returned. She was not helpless. She began to think positively, to plan.

As her mood changed she found it possible to see her

father in a different light and understand his behavior. He loved her, and feared for her. Also, his attitude was the product of his own upbringing and education. Could he help that?

She set out to search for work which would enable her to continue in school. She talked with residents of the village of Oberlin and faculty members and their wives. A church deacon in the village needed a housekeeper. She applied for the job and was hired. The deacon paid her with board and room in his home. The wife of a professor suggested that she organize and teach a drawing class for children in the village and helped her with the project. Forty children were enrolled and Nettie earned fifty cents an hour. It was enough for her tuition with a bit left over for personal needs.

She entered the theological school with James. Lucy, having graduated, went home to Massachusetts and soon was writing Antoinette about her work for the abolition of slavery and the new woman's rights movement.

In the theological school Nettie encountered professors who discriminated against her. But there were others who were won over by the young woman with the gentle blue eyes and helped her all they could.

She required no special favors, though. She did well in her studies, and despite the hours she had to devote to housekeeping and teaching she undertook a massive project. This was an exegesis, a critical explanation of Scripture. She intended to demonstrate that St. Paul was being misinterpreted by those intent on limiting the role of women.

She worked at night, beginning after her household tasks were done, often until dawn. Painstakingly she searched the Bible for material, filling page upon page with notes.

She had studied Greek as an undergraduate. Now she re-
translated the words of St. Paul from its original Greek.
Her research took months. When this was finished she began to write.

St. Paul's words to the Corinthians, she declared, were
intended primarily for the women of Corinth; they were
not intended as universal principles binding for all time.
She wrote:

"In Acts 2, verses 17 and 18, the Prophet Joel is quoted
as saying, 'And it shall come to pass in the last days, saith
God, I will pour out of my Spirit upon all flesh: and
your daughters shall prophesy, and your young men shall
see visions, and your old men shall dream dreams: and on
my servants and handmaidens I will pour out in those days
of my Spirit; and they shall prophesy. . . .'

"In the eleventh chapter of First Corinthians we learn
that females were accustomed to act as prophetesses in those
days under direct sanction of the Apostles. We have no
reason to think it was therefore unlawful for women of
that time to speak in church."

She challenged the common translation of St. Paul's in-
junction: "Let your women keep silence . . . for it is not
permitted unto them to speak."

She wrote, "*Speak* as used here is translated from the Greek
word *lalein* which means *to chatter, to make the sound of
monkeys.* Is it not, then, that St. Paul is merely cautioning
women to speak wisely and not to babble? If we are to take
his admonition literally, we should not even feel free to teach
our own children."

For thirty pages her exegesis ran on, quoting from Scripture, interpreting, explaining—a precise and logical docu-

ment which thousands of women were to utilize as the struggle of their sex for equal rights developed in the following decades.

Although it did not convince Nettie's professors, it impressed them as a tremendous feat of theological scholarship. Asa Mahan, the president of Oberlin, praised Nettie for her work and had the exegesis published in the Oberlin *Quarterly.*

The works and months passed slowly. Her time was taken up with classes, study, housework, and teaching, and what little leisure remained she spent with James. She knew now that she loved him. She was completely happy.

In the summer of 1850, with graduation only a few weeks off, Antoinette applied with the men students to the trustees for a license to preach. The license was refused her despite the urgings of several professors who declared, "Miss Brown is better qualified to wear the cloth than many of the male students." But the trustees said, "Miss Brown is a mere resident graduate pursuing the theological course, and is not a member of the theological department. Thus she needs no license from this institution and must preach or be silent on her own responsibility."

The trustees also ruled that inasmuch as she was not a registered student she would not be permitted to take part in the graduation exercises.

Nettie suffered greatly. James protested so vehemently to the trustees that his own license was jeopardized.

He pleaded with her, "Marry me, Nettie. I love you. Give this up. Let me take care of you. Please, Nettie . . ."

"No, James," she said. "I can't marry you now. Try to understand me. I must go on trying to preach."

Rejected by the school authorities, fighting a lone, unpopular battle, her need for love and support was intense. Also she loved James. She did want to marry him. But she couldn't now. He proposed again and again. Each time it was harder for her to say no.

Nettie had always known that James intended to go abroad as a missionary, but it had seemed to her something remote. Suddenly it became imminent. James told her his plans had been made; after graduation he was going home for a brief stay and then would leave for Africa.

His announcement caused a tormenting conflict. Although she had refused James's proposal she hadn't lost James. He was always nearby—loving, helping, encouraging. But soon she would lose him—unless she said yes. She lay awake at night, thinking of the man she loved. She wanted to be his wife. Without him she would feel a terrible loneliness.

Doubts beat at her brain. Perhaps she was making a mistake. Did she really have the strength to continue struggling? Perhaps they were right who said that women are weak and should look for refuge and happiness under a husband's roof. And even if she did succeed in becoming ordained—what if she found not fulfillment but emptiness without James?

With all her will she resisted the doubts. She must go on, she told herself. It might take her months to become ordained. Maybe years. If she married she might be unable to continue the struggle. No, not until she had been ordained could she think of marriage. For a few minutes she would feel conviction in her course and then a vision of James would come into her mind and the doubts would assail her again.

James' nearness, his touch, his voice, tempted her and when they met she was curt and irritable. She saw the look of puzzled hurt in his eyes and she wanted to weep for them both. She said good-by to him two days before graduation, refusing to let him kiss her, and then avoided him for the remainder of her stay at Oberlin.

She went home to the Henrietta farmhouse for the first time in four years—weary, aching with loneliness, uncertain of the future.

Here and there in America other women struggling for careers or for equal rights for their sex also were suffering hardship and disappointment. However, Antoinette Brown did not have the personality of a rebel or fighter. She merely wanted fulfillment. Her needs were to be a minister—and a wife. Born a hundred years later, she would have satisfied both needs with relative ease.

But she was born in a time when a woman could achieve a place for herself only by bitter fighting. She didn't enjoy fighting. The rage her ambition provoked made her unhappy. She was like a peaceable man who hates war but feels duty-bound to take up arms for a cause.

Her parents, good and kindly people though they were, sensed none of her needs, nor her conflict. They were too overwrought by the incredible thing she sought to do to think with understanding and sympathy. Ever since Nettie had written them from Oberlin of her intention to try to become a minister, the Squire and Mrs. Brown had believed that if she were home, if they could only talk to her, they could convince her to abandon her ambition.

They besieged her. The Squire tried to make her understand the futility of her undertaking. She would only bring pain to herself and disgrace to the family, he said. He read a letter from her brother William, now a minister with a

church of his own in Andover, Massachusetts, sternly dis-
approving of her course. Nettie felt the pain of a knife thrust
when Mrs. Brown wept that she should look to marriage for
happiness. Instantly she thought of James, gone from her
life.

Nettie's older sister Rebecca, a schoolteacher, said coldly
that if she persisted she would be looked on "as a woman of
the circus."

For weeks Nettie endured her family's criticism, pleading,
predictions of failure and disgrace. Every remark touched
on a dread or longing of her own. She did fear unhappiness
and failure. She was aware that she might disgrace her family. She did want to marry—she was in love. She was twenty-
five. At this age a woman was regarded as a spinster. Almost
all her friends were married. Soon, she thought, no man
would desire her.

The unfriendly, tense atmosphere of the home prevented
her from expressing her fears and desires, though often she
longed to put her head on her mother's lap and weep.

Only Lucy Stone, to whom she wrote often, knew of her
wretchedness. Lucy's replies gave her courage and a sense
of being linked with others struggling against prejudice,
selfishness, and dead tradition. Lucy kept her informed of
developments in the antislavery struggle and the woman's
rights movement.

In early October an exciting letter came from Lucy. A
woman's rights convention was being planned for Worcester, Massachusetts. Would Nettie come there to speak
on the status of women as set forth in Scripture? Lucy
closed by saying:

"Do not fail me, Nettie. This work is important not only

to you and to me, but to generations of women still unborn."

Nettie read the printed announcement of the convention
to her family, and Rebecca shook her head in wonderment.
"Even Ralph Waldo Emerson has signed it," she said.

Joseph Brown asked, "I suppose you intend to go?" Nettie
nodded. "I feel it is my duty."

From the East and Middle West, women and men came
to the little town of Worcester to enlist in the new cause.
Nettie met tall Susan Anthony and her devoted friend
Elizabeth Cady Stanton, Lucretia Mott, the antislavery
leader William Lloyd Garrison, and Wendell Phillips,
wealthy attorney, orator, and abolitionist. Throughout the
convention she was inseparable from Lucy Stone.

Nettie followed Sarah Tyndale, a Philadelphia merchant,
on the speaking program. Her legs trembled as she climbed
to the platform. She stood silent a moment, striving to master her fear, looking down on the faces of her audience. She
thought: "They're friendly; they have felt what I feel, they
think what I think." She felt at ease and began to speak.

"In the first chapter of Genesis, the first chapter in the
Bible, we read, 'God hath created man in His own image,
in the image of God created He him; male and female
created He them.' "

Her exegesis was as fresh in her mind as when she had
written it. She gave her own translation of the words of St.
Paul. He was cautioning the Corinthian women against
chattering in churches and not enjoining womankind to remain silent, she said. According to the words of the Prophet
Joel, she declared, women were obligated to teach, to lecture
and, if called, to preach.

She noted that many opposed to equal rights quoted

from the Bible, "Wives, submit yourself to your husbands." She added. "I think this is explained by another text, 'All be subject to one another.' "

The convention hall buzzed with approving comment of Antoinette's talk. The women particularly were impressed. There was hardly a woman present who had not writhed as an opponent of woman's rights quoted St. Paul to justify his stand. The convention elected Antoinette and Lucy to the central committee of the woman's rights organization.

A short time later Nettie was invited to take the field as a lecturer for reform—the abolition of slavery, woman's rights, and temperance. A well-to-do woman sympathizer offered to pay her expenses. Nettie accepted. She would not be serving as a minister, she thought, but undeniably she would be doing the Lord's work.

Alone she traveled throughout New England, New York, Pennsylvania, and Ohio, riding jolting stage coaches and dirty erratic trains, sleeping in slovenly taverns, eating greasy food. She spoke in a day when dramatic oratory, sweeping gestures, and table-pounding were much admired. This she shunned. She spoke naturally and simply as if to a small group of friends, communicating a warmth and liking for her audience. Like her friend Lucy and like Susan Anthony, who also were speaking in the towns and villages, she found some audiences attentive and respectful. But often she was taunted or shouted down.

Occasionally after giving a lecture she was asked to stay over and preach. This pleased her greatly. However, her preaching aroused more anger and fear than her lectures. Once a young mother hid her child's face in her skirts, crying, "Don't look at the she-devil! Don't look at her! She's evil!" In one town a man stormed out the church door, shouting, "You're not a preacher! You're just a pretty wench trying to find a husband!"

In upstate New York Antoinette was trailed by an old woman who poked her head into the hall wherever she was lecturing and shrilled, "Evil one in skirts! Blasphemer! You'll burn in hell, Antoinette Brown!" Nettie never saw the woman, only her head.

Nettie wrote Lucy of another episode which took place in the village of Brooklyn, Connecticut, where she preached one Sunday at a little Unitarian Church.

At the close of the service a man came forward, introduced himself as the deacon of the Congregational Church in Brooklyn, and invited her to preach there the following Sunday. She promised to come. When she arrived at the church the next week she was met by the minister, the Reverend George Channing. He asked her what she intended to talk about and when she told him on the status of women he said angrily, "That won't do. You'll have to preach like a man. Can you do that?"

She said she could and spent the ten minutes remaining before the start of the service thinking about a sermon. To the congregation she said she would speak on a text from the Book of John: "A new commandment I give unto ye, That we love one another; as I have loved ye, that ye also love one another. By this shall all men know that ye are my disciples."

For twenty minutes she dwelt on her theme of love and brotherhood and after the service members of the congregation surrounded her, pressed her hand and complimented her. The minister looked on in disapproval. Nettie added in her letter to Lucy:

"A few weeks later I was again preaching in Brooklyn at

the Unitarian Church. What was my surprise when the Reverend Mr. Channing invited me to hear him speak that afternoon on the text, 'Observe the Opportunity' from the Apocalypse. Imagine my further amazement when I discovered that I was the subject of his sermon, that this was the way this great and noble man made a public apology for the spirit in which he received me."

From hearing her lecture and preach, from reading about her in the reform journals and their local newspapers, a growing number of people came to know and admire the woman preacher. Men and women important in reform, in religion, in literature, and the law became her friends and took her into their homes.

Her lectures and diaries told of her friendship with such outstanding Americans as Horace Greeley, publisher of the New York *Tribune*, and his managing editor Charles Dana, Henry Thoreau, Concord's naturalist and essayist, Henry Ward Beecher, the famous New York preacher, William Lloyd Garrison, and Wendell Phillips.

Returning home for her first visit in three years, she was accorded a more cheerful reception than the one she had been given when she came back from Oberlin. Her mother and father and sister Rebecca hugged and kissed her and wanted to know all about her activities and the persons she met. They asked for her opinion on various issues and listened with respect while she spoke.

She had achieved a name for herself, and her family's fears that she would ruin her life and disgrace her home had proved baseless. Even her brother William now approved of her and invited her to preach in his church. A smaller person than Antoinette might have exulted in the situation, might have noted that once they had felt differently about her. But she said nothing of the past and felt only contentment that her home was again a place of love.

By the hour she replied to her family's questions but when the Squire or Mrs. Brown asked, "Are you happy, Nettie?" she answered briefly, "I think I am."

But privately she doubted. She preached often, yet no church had called her to its pulpit. She was still unordained. The pain of the departure of James was still great. In many lonely rooms she had thought about him, remembering his face, his voice, his gestures, wondering where he was, how he was faring.

When she visited friends she often excused herself from the adults and went to play with their children—singing them songs, telling them stories, holding the younger ones on her lap. What a richness there was in children. How wonderful it would be to have children of her own.

Was she happy? She could say yes. But a greater happiness still was denied her, she knew.

In the summer of 1853 Nettie gave a lecture in New York City. Just before she was to be introduced an usher brought her a note. It read: "Don't leave after the meeting. Want to talk to you." It was signed "Greeley." Looking around, she saw Horace Greeley and his editor Charles Dana and nodded to them.

When, after the lecture, the well-wishers had left, Greeley and Dana arose from their seats and went to meet her. They complimented her on her talk and then Greeley said, "Dana and I and some others want to keep you here in New York. You can do a lot for the slaves right here. And you can help your own sex tremendously by preaching. We're prepared to offer you a thousand dollars a year and we'll provide room

and board if you'll preach each Sunday in Metropolitan
Hall. What do you say?"

The hall seemed to spin. She felt a great happiness. This
was the fruition of her dream. This was what she had prayed
and struggled for. Metropolitan Hall was huge. With the
aid of Mr. Greeley's powerful newspaper large audiences
would be attracted to hear her preach. But she hesitated;
intuitively she felt she should wait, think.

"Mr. Greeley," she said, "you've just paid me the finest
compliment of my life. But I'd like to think about it. Can
I give you my answer tomorrow evening?"

The publisher took her hands in his. "Take all the time you
want," he said. "Only say yes."

She did not say yes. The next evening she told the two
newspapermen, "I must refuse. Please try to understand
my reasons.

"I do not want a great church in the city, row upon row
of pews, the faces of hundreds of people I don't know. I want
to know my people. I want to live with them, a small number
of people. I want to share their troubles and their happiness.
I want to be in their homes when they marry and when
their children are born. I cannot do these things here, seeing
an impersonal audience once each week.

"Mr. Greeley and Mr. Dana, please understand. I am not
being noble and sacrificing. But I know what I want. I want
to be like a shepherd with his flock."

The two men understood and Greeley said, "God bless
you, child. One day you'll have what you want."

His prediction came true. Two months later a call came to
Nettie from a church in a little town where she had once
preached. She wrote in her diary:

"I have accepted a call to the Congregational Church in South Butler, New York. It is a very poor and small church and my salary is three hundred dollars a year, ample I believe for my needs in this small community . . ."

The day of her ordination was cold, gray, and rainy, but Nettie's eyes shone with a sunshine and warmth which came from the heart. In her room in the home of one of her parishioners she put on a black silk dress and parted her dark hair. "Lord, I thank Thee for Thy blessing," she murmured.

George Caudee, a leading member of the congregation, came to escort her to the church and when he took her arm she felt the one touch of sorrow which was to intrude on the day's happiness—if only it were James by her side.

A number of Nettie's friends and co-workers were in the church, including Gerrit Smith, reform candidate for President, Herriot Hunt, a pioneer woman physician from Boston, William Henry Channing from Rochester, the Reverend Luther Lee, prominent Congregationalist from Syracuse.

Horace Greeley could not come himself but had sent two reporters.

The service began with a hymn and then Gerrit Smith told the congregation about their new minister, her kindness and goodness and strength. He spoke of her struggle against prejudice and her devotion to woman's rights and other causes of human betterment. Caudee welcomed her in behalf of the congregation and then the Reverend Lee spoke on a text she had often used herself:

"We read in the Book of Galatians: 'There is neither Jew nor Greek, there is neither bond nor free, there is neither male nor female; for ye are all one in Christ Jesus.'" In a few moments it was over—the climactic hour of her dream

—and she stood before her people, raising her hand for the benediction:

"The grace of the Lord Jesus Christ and the love of God, and the communion of the Holy Ghost be with you all. Amen."

She was a regularly ordained minister, the first of her sex in America.

She wanted, she had told Greeley, to be like a shepherd serving his flock. It didn't work out that way in South Butler. At first the difficulty was her sex. Her people, farmers and their wives, the majority with little schooling, felt awkward and inhibited toward her. They were used to taking their problems to their minister, but always the minister was a man. Even though they had called Nettie to their pulpit, their feelings about her were colored by the attitudes of the time toward women. They were inferior to men, less intelligent, weaker. The law regarded them as children. They could not vote, could not own property, could not sue or be sued; they were the wards of a father or husband.

Nettie might have won their acceptance—and in fact a small minority came to know and love her—but for her creed of a gentle and ever-loving God.

The congregation had been brought up to believe in a God who was quick to wrath, who punished fearfully. All their lives they had listened to ministers who described in graphic detail the sufferings inflicted by God on wrong-doers. They had a need to placate God, to demonstrate their fear of him. Only thus could they feel secure.

They did not believe that God was as Antoinette represented Him. Because she did nothing to arouse their fear of Him they felt uncomfortable. A few outspoken mem-

bers of the congregation urged her to preach on God's wrath
and dwell on the eternal punishment which awaited those
who sinned. She refused. She would say, "I don't believe
we are punished for our sins in the after life. Christ came
to earth to live as a man and to be crucified. Thus He atoned
for the sins of every mortal sinner. He came to us bearing a
message of hope and cheer, saying, 'The Lord is My Shepherd.' He is Christ's shepherd and our shepherd."

During the two years Antoinette spent in South Butler
her sex and her creed isolated her more and more from her
congregation. A number of her people became increasingly
angry with her and several joined other churches. Only once
did Nettie herself feel anger, and the incident which provoked it was a large factor in her decision to resign her pulpit.

During her second winter in the town she was awakened
one night by the town doctor, a member of her congregation, who asked her to accompany him on a call to a young
servant girl living alone in a hut whose baby was ill. When
the doctor and the minister arrived they found the infant
dead and the hysterical mother crying, "My baby is dead!
I want my baby—my baby! My sweet baby is going to burn
in hell. He has no name, no father. He's never been
christened."

The doctor returned home but Nettie stayed through the
night with the girl, holding her to her breast and soothing
her, "No further harm will come to your baby. Jesus loves
all little children, motherless or fatherless, white or black.
'Suffer little children to come unto Me,' He said." She left
after daybreak with a promise to conduct the funeral service
for the child.

Many of the townsfolk came to the churchyard for the
funeral and Nettie, the servant girl at her side, prayed, "Our

Shepherd in heaven, take unto Your flock this gentle lamb. Carry him in Thine arms to his resting place. Bless this young mother in her grief . . ."

The frozen lumps of earth falling on the coffin seemed to act like a signal to the onlookers. A woman cried, "Miserable sinner!" and others took it up, "Miserable sinner! She has sinned against man and God!"

Antoinette pleaded with them, "Please don't! Stop! She's only a child!" But she could not silence them. The unmarried servant girl shook with sobs. As the people finally filed from the churchyard Nettie, her lips tight with anger, announced, "Next Sunday I shall preach on the text: 'He that is without sin among you, let him first cast a stone at her.'"

She gave the sermon though there were more empty seats on Sunday than was usual. A short time later she resigned her pulpit and left the town.

She was still in South Butler when she learned of the death of James Tefft in Liberia, told in a single sentence in a letter from an Oberlin schoolmate. James was dead! She cried like a child. There was no one in the town she could share her grief with and she bore it alone, a pain and a sense of loss which diminished slowly.

While she was in South Butler one man whom she loved passed finally out of her life; and another man, who was to give her great happiness, came into it.

A short time after she heard of James's death, she was working on a sermon in her room when the landlady knocked on the door. A gentleman, the landlady announced, was downstairs in the parlor waiting to see her. Nettie made a few quick pats at her hair, straightened her dress and went to meet him. Hearing her footsteps, the man, who had been studying a portrait on the wall, turned around to greet her.

Nettie saw a short, slim man, dressed in black broadcloth, with a black beard. He smiled shyly. "Miss Brown," he said, "I'm Samuel Blackwell. I've long wanted to meet you. Besides, my sisters Ellen, Marion, and Elizabeth threatened me with all sorts of dire fates if I did not call on you when I was passing near South Butler." His sister Elizabeth was the first woman in America to receive a degree in medicine.

She liked him instantly. She led him to a horsehair sofa. Both sat down and they talked. He too believed in woman's rights, in the abolition of slavery and was active in work for these reforms. They talked about problems of reform movements, of people they both knew. Two hours sped by like minutes. When she saw him to the door he said, "Miss Brown, I hope to see you again soon. May I? She murmured, "It would please me."

She stood by the door after he left and thought: "I haven't felt happy like this in some months. Strange—it's as though I have known him a long time."

After she had resigned her pulpit she was invited to come to Cincinnati to lecture and preach. Cincinnati was where the Blackwell family lived and Samuel's mother wrote Nettie inviting her to stay with them. She did.

During the week she was there Samuel neglected his business to be with her. He escorted her to the lecture hall and the church. He sat with her in the parlor of his home. He took her to visit his friends. The day before she was to leave he took her riding in the country and blurted out, "Nettie, I love you. I want to marry you."

She blushed and stammered, "Samuel—I don't know. Samuel, I—" But she permitted him to draw her close. His lips touched her cheek. She felt a comfort and a yearning.

"Samuel," she said, "I must think on this. I'm very fond of you. But I must be sure."

He said, "Dear Nettie, I won't press you. But I'm going to see you every chance I have. And I'll write you often."

They corresponded and several times they met at reform meetings and each occasion brought Nettie happiness. Samuel was gentle, kind, and thoughtful. There was one aspect of their relationship which delighted her. Samuel's brother Henry had fallen in love with her friend Lucy Stone. A short time later they were to marry.

Nettie felt a deepening love for Samuel and one day when he said to her, "Nettie, I want to marry you, I—" she put her hand on his lips and said, "Hush, Samuel. You who believe in woman's rights don't give a woman a chance to speak. This is what I want to say—I want to marry you too."

All her life she would hear in her heart the echo of his rapturous cry, "Nettie! Nettie, my dear one!"

She was married in her home in Henrietta in a dress of white merino sewed by her sister Rebecca. Family members, friends, and relatives who had gathered for the ceremony whispered, "Nettie has never looked more beautiful." The Squire, who had told Mrs. Brown that "our daughter has fallen in love with a fine man—a fine man," performed the marriage ceremony.

When it was over Samuel gave his bride a long kiss and then Nettie's mother whispered in his ear, "Samuel, take good care of Nettie. Make her happy. She has needed you for a long time."

Nettie found great happiness and fulfillment as a wife and mother.

She who loved children bore six daughters. Always she attended first to the needs of her children; when these were met she took part in activities outside the home. The home which she and Samuel created was rich in peace and contentment.

When Nettie was a white-haired old lady her daughter Ethel said of her parents, "Their married life is a most beautiful, serene, and perfect one. Never was an unkind or angry word heard between them. Among ourselves we call Mother 'Our Calm Mountain,' and Father 'The Saint.' "

Nettie became one of the most revered women of America and tens of thousands were moved by her gospel of love. Throughout her life she was in the forefront of the woman's rights movement.

She never ceased to grow in intellect and maturity. Despite the manifold duties of a wife and mother, preacher, reform leader, and lecturer, she took up writing and published nine books and hundreds of articles.

Far into her old age she continued vigorously active. When she was 78 she went alone to the Holy Land to bring back water from the River Jordan to christen her grandchildren. At 80 she went to Alaska to preach. She finished her last book, "The Social Side of Mind and Action," when she was 93. Two years later she voted in her first Presidential election, the first in which women were permitted to take part.

Many honors were given this gentle old lady who looked, a reporter said, "like a female Lincoln." One which came from Oberlin made her very happy. Fifty-eight years after she had left the campus she was called back and awarded her Doctor of Divinity degree.

Nearing the end of her life in her ninety-seventh year, she said she felt her old friends were near her and that dying was but stepping into an adjoining room.

Alice Hamilton

In one essential Dr. Alice Hamilton was different from the first women in medicine, in law, in the ministry and in other important fields of service. The others were pioneers of their sex in established professions. Dr. Hamilton was a pioneer in a completely new field. She was the leader in the development of industrial hygiene and the prevention of occupational diseases.

In an earlier industrial age vast numbers of workers absorbed poisonous chemical particles and fumes through their skins, breathed them into their lungs, ate them with the food from their lunch boxes. Occupational diseases caused suffering, crippling, mental disorder and death.

Now in a thousand industries workers do their daily tasks in comparative safety because this slender little woman identified the diseases which plagued specific industrial occupations, traced their causes, and crusaded for prevention.

Gently reared Dr. Hamilton crawled through tunnels hundreds of feet underground to talk with coal miners and sample the air they breathed; she trod on catwalks sus-

pended over vats of acid; she studied the operations of munitions plants where a tiny spark from a shoe nail or static
electricity caused by the rustle of clothing could touch off
a devastating explosion.

What a span of life and history Alice Hamilton's years
covered.

She was born in 1869 when the memory of the Civil War
was still fresh in the minds of Americans. She was still vital
and alert in the atomic age, following with interest the
efforts of experts in industrial diseases and of scientists
studying to protect men against radiation.

It always irked Alice to list New York as her birthplace.
Fort Wayne, Indiana, where her grandfather settled when
it was an isolated post in Indian country, was to her "my
home and spiritual birthplace." But Alice was born when
Mrs. Hamilton went to New York to spend a few weeks with
her mother.

The Hamiltons lived in comfortable circumstances in a
large house with spacious grounds in Fort Wayne. Alice
was the second eldest of four sisters, all born within a six-
year period. When Alice was seventeen a boy was born into
the family.

This was not a household where the girls regarded themselves as of lower status than boys. When the baby was a
few weeks old an old German gentleman who was a friend
of the family came calling. He admired the baby and congratulated Montgomery Hamilton, his father, on having
at last begotten a son. "You should call him Primus"—
First—he said.

Mr. Hamilton looked to Edith, the oldest, for comment. She said, "Oh, no. He is only Quintus." The other girls nodded approvingly.

The boy was named Arthur but in the family circle he was always called Quintus—Fifth—or Quint.

Alice never knew her paternal grandfather, who died before she was born. But her grandmother lived in an adjoining large house—the Old House, it was called—until Alice was in her teens.

Almost every day Alice and her sisters visited their grandmother and sat with her in the comfortable library while she read from Walter Scott or Ralph Waldo Emerson or taught them about equal rights for women and the cause of temperance.

Old Mrs. Hamilton was a member of the woman's rights movement. Susan B. Anthony was her friend and stayed with her when she visited Fort Wayne. As a child Alice met the woman's rights leader and thought her ideas made a good deal of sense.

The Hamilton girls were educated by a governess and their parents. Mr. and Mrs. Hamilton also encouraged an independent pursuit of knowledge. In her teens Alice taught herself Greek and Italian—she had already learned French and Latin from her father and mother.

Mr. Hamilton stimulated in his daughters an interest in social problems and they read books about the hardships caused by the industrial revolution in England and the miseries of life in the London slums. From visitors they heard about low wages and poor working conditions in some American industries. They were shocked when one man said that workers in the steel industry worked a twelve-hour day and a seven-day week.

Poverty, social injustice, hunger, sickness—these things touched Alice Hamilton's heart. Far-off, strange places excited her. As a girl her first serious ambition was to go as a medical missionary to the Near East.

She never departed far from the essential spirit of this ambition. In her was a need to serve. She attended a finishing school in Connecticut and when it came time to decide what she would do with her life she made up her mind to become a doctor.

As a doctor, she thought, she could go anywhere—to distant countries or city slums in America—and be useful.

She studied medicine at the University of Michigan and interned at the New England Hospital for Women and Children outside Boston. Part of her work as an intern was in a dispensary conducted by the hospital in an immigrant section of Boston. Treating the under-privileged gave her much satisfaction.

Scores of times she made late night calls in rowdy sections of the city, going to tenements where children were sick, to saloons to patch up casualties of brawls and to houses of prostitution. Carrying her doctor's bag, she would walk home between midnight and dawn. "Never," she said, "did I have an unpleasant experience."

Despite the gratification she derived from treating patients, she decided against practicing medicine in a doctor-patient relationship. She was afraid she couldn't bear the pain and grief if one of her patients died.

Young Dr. Hamilton made plans to specialize in bacteriology and pathology—important medical sciences, but practiced largely in the laboratory.

In the 1890's, American training in bacteriology and

pathology was considered poor. If one wanted to be recognized as truly qualified, one had to study in Germany. Alice
Hamilton enrolled at the University of Munich.

She came away from her years in Germany with mixed
feelings. She was attracted by the warmth and kindness of
the German people but detested the antidemocratic and
militaristic views and practices of the government.

She was one of the three women students at Munich.
All were foreigners. Six German women also had applied
to the University but had been turned down. A University
spokesman told Alice the German government believed the
only reason women wanted a higher education was to equip
themselves for radical political activity.

Several faculty members made it plain they believed that
as a woman, and especially as an American woman, Alice
was incapable of serious study. But other professors were
generous with help and encouragement.

The three women students were not permitted to attend
lectures. However, Alice worked in the laboratory with
world-renowned experts and aided them in research. Occasionally there were informal lectures which she could attend. She delighted in them. They were given in charming
old-world restaurants, and the students smoked, drank beer
or coffee, or even ate supper while the professors spoke.

Alice Hamilton came home in 1896. Unable to find a
position, she enrolled at Johns Hopkins Medical School
and did research in pathological anatomy, publishing two
papers on her work.

Before a year had gone by, the Women's Medical School
of Northwestern University offered her a position teaching
pathology. She accepted eagerly. It was a chance to work in

the field in which she was trained. And the medical school was in Chicago. Hull House was in Chicago.

One night in Fort Wayne, before she entered the University of Michigan Medical School as a student Alice had gone to the Methodist Church to hear Jane Addams talk. Miss Addams had founded the famous social settlement, Hull House, about six years before, in a Chicago slum area.

Immigrants were coming to the United States in huge waves, seeking peace, freedom, and opportunity. And they filled the need of swiftly growing industries for workers.

Most Americans knew little of these millions of newcomers whose customs, languages, outlooks, and sometimes even religions were different from theirs. Later many books would be written about the immigrant peoples, telling of their fears and bewilderment in a strange land, their strivings and sufferings. But the first of these books was still to be written when Miss Addams gave her talk.

Many Americans viewed the foreigners with contempt and knew them as "Hunkies," "Dagoes," "Greasers," "Hebes," "Polacks." The newcomers were walled off by prejudice. Their great needs were ignored.

Miss Addams talked simply to her Fort Wayne audience. She didn't discuss the immigrants as a sociological abstraction. Instead she told about several families she knew in Chicago. She spoke of a father who, reacting to bitter exploitation and hopelessness, went on a violent drunk and smashed the few pieces of furniture the family had acquired through great sacrifice. She told of children whose illnesses went untreated because calling a doctor meant the family would go without bread. She told of a young girl who fled from grinding poverty to prostitution.

With her words Miss Addams created a kinship between the strangers and her native-born audience. Then she told about the work of Hull House in attempting to meet—at least in a small way—the needs of the people of the Chicago slums.

Alice Hamilton came away from the church with a dream of some day joining the company of social pioneers at Hull House.

But when she went to Chicago to teach she found that it was not easy to be taken on at the settlement house. Its residents got no salaries and even paid for their rooms and meals, but the goals of Hull House had attracted so many people that there were always more applicants than openings.

Alice was interviewed by Miss Addams, who approved of the slim, young woman doctor and said she would write her as soon as there was an opening. This did not come for a year. But it was worth waiting for. The twelve years that Alice Hamilton lived at Hull House were rich in happiness and satisfaction.

During the day on weekdays she taught at Northwestern University's Medical School. Evenings, weekends, and during summer vacations she worked for Hull House, engaging in a number of projects which best utilized her medical training.

With Julia Lathrop, another Hull House resident who later became the first Chief of the United States Children's Bureau, she went to visit a large Illinois mental hospital. They were shocked by the bleakness of the wards and the hundreds of patients in rags and filth, the soggy food, the indifference of attendants.

They made up a list of proposals and went to see the superintendent. With great tact, they pointed out how he could improve the treatment and living conditions of the patients despite his inadequate budget. A number of their proposals were accepted and carried out.

Hull House had its own day nursery for the children of mothers working or ailing, a kindergarten, public baths for men and women—few of the tenements had baths—a playground, a gymnasium, and other services and facilities commonplace today. Alice added a clinic for children, setting it up in the basement of Hull House.

After conducting the clinic for about a year she added a new service to fill a need. During the fall and winter months, she learned, few of the children got a bath. This was due both to a lack of bathtubs in working order in their homes and the belief of many immigrant mothers that bathing in the cold months was injurious. Some of the younger children brought to the clinic actually were sewed into their clothes until spring.

Alice acquired twelve small tubs. With patience and gentleness she taught the mothers the importance of bathing as an aid to health and got them to cooperate in bathing the children.

Hull House, founded in a run-down mansion, grew in size and in scope of activities. Alice Hamilton's spare-time services expanded too. She worked in adult education courses, helped foreign intellectuals who had fled from dictatorial governments find jobs, investigated the causes of a severe typhoid epidemic, and walked in picket lines of striking garment workers.

Meanwhile, she progressed in her medical work. While

teaching at Northwestern she spent two days a week doing research on the brain at the University of Chicago. In 1902 she ended her connections with Northwestern and Chicago and went to work for the newly established Memorial Institute for Infectious Diseases in bacteriological research.

She liked research—the long lonely hours in the laboratory testing, analyzing, observing changes in cultures and tissue, and the rare thrill that came with a significant finding.

Yet research lacked something. At Hull House she had a sense of service to people. In her laboratory work people were remote. She thought it would be wonderful to get into a work which would combine both aspects of her training and experience.

In 1909 a professor of sociology at the University of Chicago returned from Germany and submitted an enthusiastic report to Governor Deneen of Illinois. As a result of this report Dr. Hamilton found the answer to her dilemma.

The professor, Charles Henderson, had made a study of Germany's system of sickness insurance for workers— *Krankenkassen*. He told Governor Deneen all about it and urged him to institute it in Illinois.

The Governor was sympathetic. He decided that a study should be made of the extent and origins of industrial sickness in the state and appointed an Occupational Disease Commission to carry it out.

It was the first such study made by a state.

At the suggestion of Professor Henderson, Dr. Hamilton was appointed a member of the commission. This consisted also of the professor, four physicians, an employer, and two members of the State Labor Department. The commission was given one year to do its job.

When the commission had organized itself, it looked about for an expert to guide and supervise the work. It found that nowhere in America was there a person who could be described as an expert in occupational diseases. There was no such thing as industrial medicine. There was virtually nothing in the medical textbooks and journals about occupational diseases.

The Commission asked its woman member, Dr. Hamilton, to become managing director of the investigation. She took on the assignment. A staff of twenty—young doctors, medical students, and social workers—was engaged to help her.

At the outset Dr. Hamilton was shocked to learn that no one in Illinois knew what the occupational diseases were. The State Factory Inspector's office was directed by statute to concern itself with working conditions, but it was entirely ignorant of occupations in which workers were exposed to disease.

The Commission decided to investigate the lead and brass trades, the problem of carbon monoxide in the steel mills, caisson disease—which afflicted workers in tunnels when they went too quickly from compressed air to normal air pressure—and two or three other maladies.

In addition to directing the general program, Dr. Hamilton made herself responsible for the investigation of lead poisoning.

Excepting carbon monoxide, which probably began to take a toll of human life as soon as primitive man discovered fire, lead is doubtless the oldest of the industrial poisons. Dr. Hamilton learned that the ancient Romans knew of its dangers. Their writers termed it "a disease of slaves," for it was slaves who worked with lead.

Lead poisoning may cause palsy, paralysis, coma, mental breakdown, convulsions, and death.

Dr. Hamilton assigned part of her young task force to reading hospital records, talking with union officials, and interviewing doctors and pharmacists in working-class districts. She wanted to find out how widespread were the casualties from lead poisoning.

They were widespread indeed. She and her group found lead trades they never knew existed: the making of freight-car seals; polishing of cut glass; making of coffin trim; the wrapping of cigars in tin foil, which was really lead.

She studied one small lead plant with eighty-five workers. In six months thirty-five of them had been infected with lead poisoning.

She interviewed scores of "leaded" workers to learn more about the disease. To find a particular worker was often a wearying task of detection.

In a plant her manner with workers was direct and friendly. It wasn't a manner she adopted for the occasion; she was being herself. Mostly the workers trusted her. While at Hull House she had learned some Russian and Polish, and this was a great help.

In a plant a worker would tell her that Stanislaus—or Angelo or Gregor—was sick at home. Yes, the worker thought the absent man was leaded. Stanislaus what? What was his last name? The worker shrugged. He didn't know. Men came and went. There was no time for talk.

Usually the employer couldn't help her either. Employment records were inadequate then. The employer didn't even have to know the last names of his men for salary purposes, for he paid them in cash, not by check.

Dr. Hamilton might emerge from the plant with an approximation of the absent worker's last name. Someone might also know the district where he lived. Someone else might give her a description of the man.

With the slenderest of clues she would go from street to street, knocking on tenement doors, inquiring of priests and ministers and grocers and saloonkeepers.

Most times she found her man. She would examine him in the kitchen of his flat, surrounded by silent children awed by the lady doctor and her strange instruments, and question him about conditions in the plant where he worked.

There were instances when the man she sought was not so sick that he couldn't leave his house, and she conducted her examination where she finally found him—in a corner of a foreign language club or a union hall, or in the back room of a saloon.

Sometimes the people she wanted to help tried to fool her. She would locate the flat of a lead-sick worker. And the man's wife, suspicious of a stranger, would pretend that the man didn't live there.

There were also employers who tried to trick her.

Her task force located a Polish workman in a Chicago hospital, suffering from colic and palsy. Dr. Hamilton talked with the man. He said he worked in a plant where enamel was applied to bathtubs. This was a lead trade she had never heard of. She wanted to see it.

At the plant the owner scoffed at the workman's story. The workman, he said, was most likely suffering from too much drinking, not lead poisoning. And if by chance the man did have lead poisoning he hadn't contracted it at work because no lead was used in coating the bathtubs.

Seeing her doubt, the owner said, "Come. I'll show you the workroom and you'll see for yourself." She saw a dozen

or so Polish workers applying enamel paint to metal bathtubs. She talked with them. None had ever had symptoms
of lead poisoning.

Persisting, she wrote down the name of the paint and went
to the factory which made it. There she was told that no
lead is used in enamel paint.

She went back to see the sick workman and told him what
she had found. "Trick," the Pole said. "Boss, he trick. You
no see enameling. He show you touch up." The enameling
process, he explained, was carried on in another part of
the plant.

Once more she went to the plant and at her request was
taken to the enameling room. There she saw finely ground
enamel being dusted on to red-hot tubs, melting and covering
their surface. The air was heavy with enamel dust. This
dust, she found, contained a high proportion of red oxide
of lead.

The findings of the Occupational Disease Commission
were fruitful. Reports were submitted to the governor on
lead and brass poisoning, the causes and effects of carbon
monoxide poisoning in the steel mills, on 161 cases of
caisson disease, on boiler makers' deafness, and on an eye
disease of coal miners known as nystagmus.

Alice Hamilton's lead report was of special importance.
In it she identified a number of lead trades not previously
recognized as dangerous. She also dealt with the process of
lead infection.

At the time she wrote, and for some years thereafter, it
was commonly believed that lead poisoning was caused by
the failure of workmen to wash their hands and scrub their
fingernails; then lead particles were transmitted to the food
which they put in their mouths. She expressed the con-

viction that poisoning derived from breathing lead dust and fumes. (Her belief was later confirmed by experimentation.) She declared that the air must be kept clear for effective hygiene.

The Commission reports resulted in the enactment of a workman's compensation law by the State of Illinois. It provided that workmen who were made ill or were injured or incapacitated as a result of their work would receive small financial benefits.

It was the first such law in America.

With the submission of its reports to Governor Deneen, the Commission's work was done. But Dr. Hamilton's was just beginning. She undertook what was virtually a one-woman campaign against industrial disease in America. This is how it happened.

While the Illinois investigation was going on, the Commission decided to send its director to Brussels for the fourth International Congress on Occupational Accidents and Diseases.

Authorities on industrial hazards from Germany, England, Italy, the Netherlands, France, and Austria-Hungary read papers. Dr. Hamilton was appalled at how little was known in America about the hazards of which these representatives spoke. When it came to hygienic measures, America was even farther behind.

"The meeting hurt my national pride," Dr. Hamilton said later.

There were only two papers by Americans. A Major Ashford reported on hookworm infestation in Puerto Rico and Dr. Hamilton gave a paper on her study of the lead industry.

After she spoke, other delegates questioned her. What was the incidence of lead poisoning in a certain industry?

What was the death rate? She couldn't answer. Nobody in America knew.

She was asked to tell about laws and regulations for the dangerous trades in America. She had to answer that there weren't any.

An official of the Belgian Labor Bureau halted the questioning. "It is a fact," he said, "that there is no industrial hygiene in America."

There was a third American at the meeting, Charles O'Neill, United States Commissioner of Labor. He introduced himself to Dr. Hamilton and questioned her closely about her work for the Illinois Commission.

"I am appalled at our backwardness in industrial hygiene," he said. "When I return to Washington I am going to try to do something about it."

Dr. Hamilton said, "I'm glad. I don't know of anything that more needs doing."

She wondered at the meaning of the odd look he gave her. Some weeks later when she was in Illinois she found out.

She got a letter from the Labor Commissioner. He asked her to become a Federal agent assigned to investigate occupational poisoning, starting with lead. Her field would be the entire United States.

If she accepted, O'Neill added, she would have to find out herself what occupations were dangerous and where the plants were. She would have to determine the methods of investigation. Moreover, she would have to carry out her investigations without legal authority to compel an employer to cooperate or even to admit her to his plant. She would have to persuade employers to help.

She accepted the assignment. When the Illinois study

was completed she went to work for the United States Government.

Her previous investigation of the lead trades had only scratched the surface. Now she explored the basic lead industries, the processing of lead itself, in smelters and refineries from New York to Colorado.

Early in her work she broadened her function. It was not enough, she decided, merely to investigate and report to Washington. Years might go by before her recommendations resulted in reform. Meanwhile, men would sicken and die. She resolved to try to improve conditions whenever she saw the chance. She had no legal support for this, so she relied on reason and "the innate goodness of people."

One of her most important voluntary reforms was achieved in the large National Lead Company. Inspecting several of its lead-producing plants in Illinois, she found the air thick with dust and fumes from piles of lead and roasting furnaces. What she saw she noted for her report to Washington.

When Edward Cornish, President of the National Lead Company, came to visit one of his Illinois plants she went there to see him. She was sure, she told him, that his men were being poisoned.

Cornish was angry and indignant. "Dr. Hamilton," he said, "the National Lead Company plants are models of their kind. They are modern in every respect. To be blunt, I don't believe you. We have never had reports of lead poisoning. Yet you spend a brief time in our plants and declare our men are being leaded."

She said, "I am sure, Mr. Cornish."

The president glared at her. "Come with me, please," he

said. He led her out of the office and to one of the work-rooms. He halted a passing workman. "See here," he said, "did the lead ever make you sick?" "No, not sick," the man stammered. "Never sick."

Cornish demanded, "Any other men sick? Any other men leaded?" The workman was shaking his head. "No, no men sick. All good. All strong."

Cornish turned to Dr. Hamilton. "You heard. That is the testimony of a man who works here. I told you we don't have any lead poisoning."

"You're mistaken," she said. "Your men are breathing lead dust and fumes—they're breathing poison. Poison makes people sick."

He shook his head in surrender to her stubbornness. "All right, Dr. Hamilton. All right. I'm sure your belief is without basis. But I'll give you a chance to prove you're right. You come back with proof that my men are being poisoned and I'll make any changes you think are necessary."

She again did the detective work she had performed in her lead investigation for the Illinois Commission. Alone, without an officer of the company present, she talked with workmen in the plant. From them she got clues to other workmen they thought were sick with lead poisoning. She trailed the latter to their homes and to hospitals.

The next time Cornish came to Illinois she presented him with the medical records of twenty-two of his employees sick with lead poisoning of such severity that they had to be hospitalized.

The man did even more than he had promised.

He put engineers to work in the company's Illinois plants to devise methods and equipment for dust and fume control. When these were completed, instructions and blue-prints were sent to other plants of the National Lead Company in other states.

While this work was going on Dr. Hamilton asked Cornish to take a further step against industrial disease.

"Even with the best air control system," she told him, "there will be some leakage of lead dust. You should give your workers a medical examination once a week to check for lead absorption."

This made good sense to the industrial leader, and he ordered that a medical department be established in each of his company's plants. Industrial medicine was growing.

In her work Dr. Hamilton also functioned as a one-woman information bureau, telling executives in a given industry about the occupational safeguards that had been worked out by a fellow-executive elsewhere.

She was greatly concerned about the absence of precautions in the sandblasting operation in the sanitary-ware industry. She saw men sandblasting bathtubs, wash basins, and toilet bowls in rooms so heavy with dust that no lighting could dispel the murky twilight. Many of the workmen fell ill of a severe lung infection.

In Sheboygan, Wisconsin, she went into a sanitary-ware plant and saw with elation that the owner had largely eliminated the hazard. In this plant the sandblasting was done in airtight chambers which kept the dust from pervading the rest of the establishment. These chambers were given frequent cleaning and airing. The men who worked in them wore face masks with respirators. They breathed fresh air piped in from the outside to the respirators.

Thereafter whenever she went into a sanitary-ware plant

or another kind of establishment which used sandblasting, she told the owner or manager about the system she had seen in Sheboygan.

She also appeared before legislative committees in a number of states and urged passage of laws to enforce hygienic measures in dangerous trades, workmen's compensation and accident insurance. In several states she was a major force in getting such legislation adopted.

After two or three years Alice Hamilton knew that in industrial medicine she had found her life's work. "It had the challenge and excitement of exploration," she said. "Moreover, much of what I discovered was useful to human well-being."

There was only one thing she held more important than the cause for which she worked. That was the cause of peace. The outbreak of World War One in Europe in 1914 made her heartsick. When, the following year, Jane Addams went to The Hague to preside over an international congress of women protesting the war Alice Hamilton went with her as one of an American delegation of fifty.

Miss Addams urged the women from a dozen and a half countries to do more than protest, to try to gain a peace. She proposed a plan for "continuous mediation" under which representatives of neutral nations would make repeated offers to the warring countries for a peace pact.

The congress adopted the proposal. A Boston woman, Emily Balch, was elected to visit Russia and the Scandinavian countries to try to get approval of government officials and other influential persons for the mediation plan.

Miss Addams was elected to visit eight other countries, and Alice Hamilton went with her.

Making long detours to avoid battlefronts and rail centers and harbors essential to military operations, the two women traveled to England, France, Germany, Austria-Hungary, Switzerland, the Netherlands, Belgium, and Italy.

Some officials and important private citizens said that personally and privately they welcomed the plan. Some were indifferent. Some were opposed. Essentially the two Americans could find no firm support for "continuous mediation."

Only one man was eager to see it tried but, as he said, "I do not represent a government." He was Pope Benedict XV, who received the two American women in a private audience in the Vatican in Rome.

The forty-minute interview was conducted in French, with Alice translating the Pope's words for her friend. His Holiness told of his deep grief over the war. Commenting on the peace plan, he said, "It is the most promising undertaking I have heard of. I will pray for your success."

The two women sailed back to the United States. Jane Addams went to see President Woodrow Wilson in an unsuccessful effort to induce him to mediate in the conflict. Alice Hamilton, saddened by the failure of the plan and the continuing war, immersed herself in work.

The United States was supporting the Allies—England, France, and Russia. Soon it would enter the war against Germany and Austria-Hungary. Meanwhile, the Allies were appealing frantically to the United States to become their arsenal. Their armies and navies were using thousands of tons of munitions daily, much faster than their own industries could manufacture them.

The United States responded. Munitions plants were

hastily erected and from them began to come mountains of shells and mines and the explosives with which to fill them.

America had relied mainly on Germany for the chemicals used in explosives. Now a vast military chemical industry quickly sprang up. This industry used or created scores of gases, acids, and chemicals, many dangerous to health and life.

Because the manufacturing processes were new to America and the plants were erected with great urgency there were few safeguards against the dangers. And there was little knowledge in America about how the gas, acid, and chemical poisons acted on the human body.

Shortly after she returned from Europe Dr. Hamilton was assigned by the Labor Department to study the occupational dangers of the wartime chemical industry.

Her work would be dangerous. She was still without authority to compel a plant management to cooperate or even to admit her; she would have to depend on her tact and persuasion. And whether as a result of military secrecy, or of poor liaison between the military agencies of the government and the Labor Department, she was unable to get a list of plants and their locations.

She knew though that most of the plants were located along the Atlantic coast and that a number were in New Jersey. She went to New Jersey. In a little railroad station in a small town she got a clue to the location of nearby plants manufacturing nitric and picric acids and nitrocellulose.

The eyes of the dozen or so people waiting for a train were all on two men. She thought first they were circus clowns. They were grotesque. Their clothing was bedaubed with yellow. Their hair was streaked with yellow. The color had stained their faces, deepening in the hollows under the eyes and above the chin, and their hands.

No, these were not clowns. But what were they? One of the two men saw that she was curious. "We're canaries, lady," he said.

She was puzzled. "You mean you work in a dyeing plant?"

He grinned. "No, lady, we work in the Canary Islands." He pointed out the window to factories in the distance. "That's what we call them. We make picric acid for the French."

She asked, "Is it dangerous?"

The workman answered, "That's why we're leaving. When they're making the acid there's an explosion sometimes and an orange smoke comes out. You breathe it. It doesn't burn much. You don't think too much about it. But a little later you're dead."

The second man said, "That's right. A feller I roomed with, he died. The stuff's like poison gas."

She walked to the nearest plant across once-rich farm land, the spring grass blackened by chemical fumes, trees naked of leaves and withered. A brook was discolored with chemicals and stank acridly. She, a pacifist, thought sadly, this is what happens when man turns to war.

The plant consisted of several giant sheds. One housed the managers and the office staff. She obtained a permit there and inspected the operations and talked with executives, foremen, and workmen.

The workmen and foremen looked as though they had been showered with yellow paint. Acid had eaten holes in their clothing and their skin showed in patches, colored yellow.

She spent a number of days in the area studying plants producing acids and nitrocellulose. She saw nitric acid, a dangerous caustic, being made in tightly covered mixing vats.

Whenever nitric acid comes in contact with organic material or water it gives up nitrous fumes. In the vats used in the primitive operations of the time, the fumes built up tremendous pressure.

In one day she saw eight vats burst into pieces and she fled with the workmen into the outdoors ahead of the rolling clouds of orange fumes.

Doctors then knew little about the dangers of nitrous fumes. Dr. Hamilton studied the cases of five men who had died from the fumes. In a typical case a workman was exposed to heavy fumes for a brief time. He choked, his face turned blue. But when he got into the fresh air and breathed deeply his distress disappeared. Seemingly he had no lasting ill effects.

Then, some hours later, the workman was stricken. It was like a tight band across his chest, he told fellow roomers. They saw him gasping, trying to draw air into his lungs. In minutes he was dead.

In cases of milder exposure the fumes often caused pneumonia. Some of the workmen had arrested cases of tuberculosis. Inhalation of the fumes reactivated the disease.

In most plants, she reported to Washington, engineers were striving to create safeguards but there would be many casualties before these were perfected.

From New Jersey, Alice Hamilton went to Virginia to

visit a chemical plant. In the town of Hopewell, on the James River, the du Pont Company had built an excellently operated plant employing 12,000 workers in the manufacture of nitrocellulose. Nearby the company had put up a model village for its all-male working force.

Many of the younger men wanted excitement, not available in the du Pont village. It was available in plenty in a wide-open town across the river, with saloons which never closed, gambling rooms, and dance halls.

Alice Hamilton came to Hopewell with a woman friend. There were no rooms for women in the model village. Nor were there fit rooms in the town across the river. After a tiring search, they found a room down river in an abandoned steamboat converted into a rooming house.

For meals they had to go into the town across the river, where knifings, shootings and brutal beatings were nightly occurrences. Prostitutes were numerous. Eating dinner in a Greek restaurant, Dr. Hamilton and her friend saw a du Pont policeman eying them suspiciously. They couldn't understand why.

The next day when Dr. Hamilton went to the plant the manager explained. He said with a smile, "One of our policemen turned in a report on you and your friend. He thought you might be—er, er—that is, immoral ladies."

She visited several plants manufacturing nitroglycerine. Usually they were built between high hills which would contain the force of an explosion if a plant blew up.

"I don't think that anything I experienced before frightened me so much as this," she said. Yet she insisted on seeing everything.

In one plant she went with the manager into a small

room where nitroglycerine was pouring in a thick syrupy stream from a pipe into a large bin.

"Almost anything can cause this stuff to blow up," the manager said.

He called her attention to a tank of water under the bin. "If the temperature of the nitro shoots up," he said, "we dump the whole thing into the water."

He said to a workman, "How's the static?" The workman passed his hand over the bin. "About as usual," he said.

The manager explained that the greatest danger of an explosion came from a spark which static electricity could cause, or the nail on a shoe. He walked with her to a window and pointed to a chute going down three floors to the ground. "If someone yells 'spark,'" he said, "you run for that window and dive into that chute. And when you hit the ground don't turn around—just keep running."

In 1917 the United States went to war. The military chemicals industry expanded. Dr. Hamilton's work became even more important. She was given a staff of chemists, doctors, and physical scientists to help her. In Washington the National Research Council established a committee of experts to aid her as consultants.

Her reports and those of the committee were too late to reform conditions in World War One. But they provided a basis for improvements which came later. By the time of the Second World War, most of the dangers, including new ones arising from new processes, had been eliminated. By then the United States Public Health Service had a branch concerned exclusively with industrial poisons. The Department of Labor had a section which helped in solving engineering problems, and the Army and Navy also had their medical, scientific, and engineering experts.

When World War One was over, Dr. Hamilton explored the limestone industry and its lethal clouds of stone dust, the granite industry, where workers were exposed to a disease of the lungs known as silicosis, and the brass and copper industries.

Industrial medicine and hygiene had arrived. Their importance was recognized in medicine, industry, and government. A number of doctors were specializing in the field. They wrote papers on their findings and held meetings to discuss their problems and experiences. But the number was not sufficient to meet the growing demand. As yet there was nowhere in America a training center for industrial medicine.

It was the Harvard University Medical School which was the first school to provide training in industrial medicine and hygiene. Harvard began to look for an outstanding person to direct this training.

By a person, Harvard really meant a man. For the University, approaching the 300th anniversary of its founding, had never had a woman on its faculty. Now Dr. David Edsall, Dean of the Medical School, made up his mind that if Harvard wanted a truly outstanding person the traditional exclusion of women would have to be ended.

He was sure that the best qualified person in America was Dr. Alice Hamilton—if only she would accept the post.

To his great satisfaction, she did accept when it was offered her. She recognized the strong need for trained people and she decided she could be more useful to industrial medicine by teaching it at Harvard than by continuing in the field. And Harvard said she could continue to do some work in industry.

Her appointment was approved by the Harvard Corporation, the administrative body of the university. But because of her sex the corporation was not altogether happy about it.

At a meeting of the corporation, one member inquired anxiously if Dr. Hamilton would insist on getting a professor's quota of tickets for the Harvard football games. Harvard was a football power then and tickets were in great demand. The question was relayed to Dr. Hamilton and she promised that she would never insist on football tickets.

Another member was worried that Dr. Hamilton might demand to use the Harvard Club in Boston. At the time the Club did not even admit wives or daughters of members. Dr. Hamilton said that she wouldn't insist on this either.

She was fifty when she started to teach at Harvard.

The years flew. She began with a handful of students. The number grew rapidly. Then, attracted by her reputation, students came to Harvard from foreign lands where industrialization was developing—from Turkey, China, the Philippines, Egypt, Argentina, and Brazil. After completing their training these students went home, and as time passed wrote to Dr. Hamilton about how they were dealing with industrial dangers in their countries and asked for her advice on problems.

Dr. Hamilton made her home in Boston's Back Bay. She made good friends and was happy. But many people regarded her as a radical because she was outspoken against any encroachment on civil liberties and urged the cause of trade unionism.

When she first came to Harvard a number of persons attacked her as "pro-German." This was because she was speaking at public meetings to raise funds for a campaign of the Quakers to feed hungry German children. When some of these persons protested to Harvard, Dr. Edsall said, "Harvard cherishes academic freedom. Dr. Hamilton is doing what her conscience dictates."

During her years at Harvard, Dr. Hamilton studied carbon monoxide dangers in the coal mines, the mercury-producing industries, the dye-producing industries and others. Somehow she always found time for more work. For ten years she served as medical consultant to the General Electric Company.

She spoke at a number of international congresses on industrial medicine and occupational dangers. She served as a consultant to the Labor Department.

In 1935, when she was 67 years old, Harvard appointed her Professor Emeritus, and she retired—but only from Harvard. She settled in a spacious and gracious old house in the Connecticut village of Hadlyme and took on assignments when she was in her seventies.

A few months before the outbreak of World War Two Dr. Hamilton attended a meeting on occupational diseases in Germany as a representative of the Labor Department. What she observed in Germany and heard from German friends in science deepened the detestation she already felt for Nazism. And when America prepared to enter the war against Nazism and Fascism she felt impelled to lay aside her pacifist philosophy.

"We must get down into the arena and throw our strength to the right side," she said.

At the age of 89 Alice Hamilton sat with an interviewer in the living room of her cozy house in Hadlyme. A few feet away the water of the Connecticut River lapped at the lawn grass.

She had just returned from voting in the town elections and the exercise had put color into her face. In moccasins she seemed tiny. She still was as slender as a girl, as erect.

Did she still play any part in industrial medicine?

"No," she said. "My only association with it is through former students who sometimes write to me, and the professional journals. There are seven now concerned with industrial poisons and other dangers. I read them all to learn what is going on."

Have the problems of industrial poisons been solved?

"No. I don't think they can ever be solved for once and for all. You see, new industries, new materials, new processes often create new dangers.

"The great problem now is how to dispose safely of atomic waste material. The British put it in steel and cement containers which they lower deep into the sea. But many, many years from now these containers will yield up their poisons. Then what?

"I read all the reports and discussions"—she motioned toward a pile of journals on a table—"but there's no answer yet.

"I worry about it. But I keep hoping. Maybe tomorrow or the next day will bring a solution."

In her ninetieth year she was looking to tomorrow—with hope.

Lillian M. Gilbreth

LILLIAN MOLLER and Frank Gilbreth had no more than a dozen days together before they were married. They met for the first time on a June evening in 1903 in the Boston Public Library at Copley Square.

Lillie was spending a few days in Boston sight-seeing before sailing for a tour of Europe. Her chaperone, who was Frank Gilbreth's cousin, introduced them.

Lillie was then twenty-five, Gilbreth ten years older. She was a native of California, he of Maine. Although they were as unlike as the two states they were instantly attracted to each other.

She was slight, almost frail. He was tall, with a strong body hardened by laborer's work. She had been carefully sheltered in a home of wealth. She was a graduate of the University of California. At seventeen he had passed the entrance examination at Massachusetts Institute of Technology, then decided he did not want to burden his widowed mother with his support for four more years and went to work as a bricklayer.

Lillie's interests were books, music, reading, and writing

poetry. Gilbreth, a dynamo of energy, ideas, and ambitions, had become a construction foreman at nineteen and a superintendent at twenty-two, meanwhile mastering the trades of bricklaying, carpentry, stonework, tinsmithing, and roofing. When they met he was a self-taught engineer and one of the biggest individual contractors in America.

Gilbreth was handsome and charming—and knew it. She was pretty, her voice was soft and pleasing, but she was certain she was too unattractive to win a husband.

She had never gone anywhere, unchaperoned, with a man who was not a relative until Gilbreth took her to dinner and the theater during their courtship. But he was often in the company of handsome women. His friends used to say that Gilbreth liked to take girls driving in his buggy "with the reins wrapped around the whip"—leaving his hands free.

Lillie was shy and a little anxious with strangers. He was utterly sure of himself in any setting. He liked to joke in a way which attracted attention to himself. Like the time he came to the quiet and dignified Moller home in Oakland, California.

Lillie and her father and mother, two very correct parents whom Frank had met for the first time in New York when Lillie came back from Europe, received him at the door. Mr. Moller said they would all have tea in the sunroom. Just over the threshold of the living room Gilbreth halted, his blue eyes glinting with humor.

A workman, his back to the group, was building a new fireplace. Gilbreth looked on for a moment, then said loudly, "Now there's an easy job, laying brick. It's dead easy. I don't know why they pay bricklayers so much."

The workman's back stiffened; his neck turned red. Mr. Moller coughed gently and put his hand on Gilbreth's sleeve. Gilbreth said cheerfully, "It seems to me that all you do is pick up a brick, slap some of that stuff on it and lay it down. Dead easy."

The bricklayer turned and looked carefully at the fashionably dressed visitor. "Dead easy, eh, mister?" he said. "Why don't you try it?" He held out his trowel.

Gilbreth took the tool in one hand. With the other he picked up a brick, tossed it a few times to examine its sides, applied mortar with a swift rotary motion, scraped off the excess and tapped the brick in place. Immediately he picked up another brick and began the procedure anew. The workman seized his hand.

"That's enough, you old bricklayer," he shouted and slapped Gilbreth on the back. "You're dressed like a dude but you've laid many thousands of bricks." Gilbreth grinned and wiped his hands with a handkerchief.

Lillie came to expect anything of him. On a later visit to her home he abruptly broke off a conversation with her parents. "Excuse me," he said, "I think Miss Lillie would look nicer up here." He lifted her out of her chair and sat her on top of a china closet, resuming the conversation while she strove for dignity and safety on her perch.

To her surprise, she fell in love with him. To her greater surprise, he fell in love with her. But what surprised her most of all was that her correct parents also loved him. "He's like a breath of fresh air," Mrs. Moller said happily.

Lillie Moller, who had six times been a bridesmaid was married in her parents' home in 1904. College-educated women were looked on then as somewhat odd and the Oakland newspaper felt it necessary to assure its readers that "although a graduate of the University of California, the bride is nonetheless an extremely attractive young woman."

To retiring, bookish Lillie Gilbreth—how strange her new name sounded—her husband was like a man from another world. He believed that he could do almost anything and he helped her to see that her own limitations were largely self-made and that she herself could unmake them.

He jeered at the prevailing view that women were delicate beings inferior to men in brains and ability. They are capable of doing all that men do, he told Lillie.

Frank, who had marched in a parade in New York dramatizing the demand of women for the vote and other rights, added that a woman owed it to herself and society to make the most of her capabilities.

The train carrying Frank and Lillie on their honeymoon was hardly out of sight of San Francisco when he began to explain his philosophy of marriage. They would be partners, he told Lillie, in the home, in the raising of a family, in work.

Lillie, adoring this husband of hers who spoke so confidently, nodded. Quickly she agreed to the terms and goals of the partnership as he proposed them.

"I think," Gilbreth said, "that we should have a large family. Twelve children would be just right. Yes, twelve children—six boys and six girls."

Lillie said, "That will be nice, Frank," and he beamed.

They did have six boys and six girls.

"Now, Mrs. Pied Piper," he said, "let's discuss work." He suggested that Lillie work with him in construction and engineering; he would teach her. However, if this did not appeal to her, he said, he would give up his work and join

her in whatever she wanted to do. Like writing. Lillie protested she could not ask him to give up the work in which
he had invested so much of himself and with such good
results. She would work with him, she said.

"Good," he said, and there in the railroad car he began
her education. "First I want to tell you about concrete and
masonry," he said. " 'Bond' is the term we use to illustrate
the relationship of joints in masonry . . ."

Frank maintained permanent offices in New York and
Boston. He and Lillie rented an apartment in New York
overlooking the Hudson River. They had a few days together, then he took a field trip to one of his construction
jobs. When he returned he had photographs and plans
with him and in the evenings he interpreted them to his
wife.

He explained problems of stress, told of the mixing of
cement, described the various tools used by building trades-
men. He bought for Lillie textbooks on engineering and
read them with her, sketching illustrations to clarify points.

Soon Lillie was accompanying him on field trips, relating
plans she had seen in her living room to foundations, walls,
beams and roofs. When Frank said, "It's not dangerous if
you watch your footing," she walked out on scaffolding
fifteen floors above the ground. She hefted tools and once
at his urging learned to run a small steam engine.

Her mind was eager and she surprised Frank with the
swiftness of her learning. Coming to construction projects
with eyes undisciplined by formal training and routine, she
sometimes saw defects which had escaped Frank, and better
ways of doing things.

Gilbreth, a man of large ego, did not easily accept sug-
gestions from a novice, even if she was his wife. He found,

however, that she was amazingly stubborn when she thought she was right. She persisted until he accepted her suggestion or was able to convince her that it was unsound.

It amused Lillie that he found it difficult to acknowledge that she was right in a difference of opinion. Instead he would expound to her as his own idea something which she had suggested a few days before.

Invariably he would later own up to his transparent trick and sigh, "I can't help it, Lillie. I'll try not to do it again."

But in one important area he readily admitted her superiority—in understanding of the human factor in work, in human relationships.

She possessed a rare insight into the individual emotional needs of those with whom she came in contact. At college she had taken courses in the new science of psychology, which added to her understanding of people.

When Frank sometimes became exasperated because a key workman seemed unable to master a new task, Lillie was able to perceive that the man was emotionally unsuited for it and to suggest other work more compatible to his personality.

Her capacity for understanding the needs of people would become of tremendous value in a new field into which Frank was to lead her and in which they would both succeed. Meanwhile the babies began to come. Anne was the first.

Babies, Frank said, begin learning from birth, so he sat Anne's bassinet on a desk in her parents' bedroom where she could hear them talk about construction. A German nurse employed to care for Anne protested, "She's only an infant. She can't understand a thing you say."

"How do you know?" Frank retorted. "And please talk

only German in front of the baby. I want her to know English *and* German."

He ruled that no baby talk would be uttered in Anne's hearing because "the only reason a baby talks like a baby is that he's heard nothing else from adults."

A week later Lillie awoke at night and saw Frank leaning over Anne. She heard him whisper, "Is ee a ittle bitty baby? Is ee Daddy's itty bitty girl?"

Lillie smiled. "Whom are you talking to, Frank?" she said.

Each year there was another baby. After Anne came Mary, then Ernestine, then Martha. Frank introduced the girls to visitors as "my harem" and added with feigned sadness, "I'm the last of the Gilbreths, the last male of the line." Then he'd say to Lillie, "It's all right, dear, I know you're doing the best you can."

Child number five was a boy. After he came into the world Frank kissed his wife and said, "Good work, Lillie. I think this one we'll keep. What shall we name him?" She did not often joke and, exhausted from the childbirth, she was half asleep, but she could not resist the temptation. "How about naming him Next-to-the-Last-of-the-Gilbreths?" she said.

Now at the crowded dinner table Frank would tease, "The first four were just practice, Boss, but I suppose we might as well keep them. They'll probably come in handy to scrub the pots and pans." Shrieking, the four little girls would rush him and Frank would let himself be wrestled to the floor.

William was born while the family lived in Providence, Rhode Island. After he was born Lillie enrolled at Brown

University and earned a doctorate in psychology. She and Frank felt that the additional training in psychology was of utmost importance because they were now deeply involved in the new science of industrial engineering. In those days it was better known as scientific management. The Gilbreths had a simple definition for scientific management: the one best way of doing work.

This science was born in the minds of a small group of men shortly before the twentieth century. They were appalled by crude and inefficient managerial practices and the waste of human resources.

They began to study industrial practices, and they thought and experimented. As they acquired knowledge and experience they began to write papers for engineering journals and talk to management groups. They explained, for instance, how the output of a plant could be raised simply by scientific organization of its equipment and facilities, so that raw materials proceeded in a straight line through the successive machines processing it, without detours and interruptions. They concerned themselves with methods of training workers and foremen in their jobs. They saw that excessive fatigue lessened output and wore out the workers and they occupied themselves with learning how to reduce fatigue. Some of the scientific management pioneers also sought to improve labor-employer relations, stressing that satisfied workers were more efficient workers.

Frank Gilbreth was among the pioneers of scientific management. He brought original contributions to the new field. One of the most important of these was motion study.

He was only a boy when he began groping for the one

best way of doing work. Following his graduation from
Boston English High School he got a job as a bricklayer's
apprentice and was assigned to a journeyman bricklayer
named Tom.

Tom, he observed, used three sets of motions in laying
bricks—one when he was working slowly, a second when
he was working in high speed, and a third when he was
demonstrating the craft to his apprentice.

The boy called this to Tom's attention and the latter
scratched his head. He had never noticed it. Frank watched
other bricklayers. Each used a different set of motions,
sometimes more than one set. He mused on this awhile,
then went to his foreman. "Did you ever notice that no
two of the men lay bricks the same way?" he said. "That's
important because if one man is doing the job the right
way then all the others are doing it the wrong way. Now if
I had your job I'd find out who's laying brick the easiest
and fastest way and make all the others copy him."

"If you had my job," the foreman shouted, "you'd lay a
brick in the mouth of an apprentice who went around giving advice."

Frank kept silent thereafter but while learning to lay
bricks he experimented with various motions, seeking a
system which would be most productive and least fatiguing.

Later, as a foreman, he constantly sought ways of speeding work by eliminating waste motions and cutting down
fatigue. As a youthful superintendent his interest led him
to the invention of a unique motion-saving device.

Supervising the construction of walls, Frank saw how
tiring it was for the bricklayers on the scaffolds to stoop and
stretch. The taller the walls grew the lower the men had to

stoop to pick up bricks and mortar and the higher they had to stretch to lay the bricks. It would be possible, he told himself, to design a scaffold which would eliminate many of the motions.

Evenings at home he created such a scaffold. It was adjustable in height. As a wall grew, workmen could raise the scaffold without interrupting the work of the bricklayers. The scaffold also held conveniently placed platforms for bricks and mortar. It eliminated stretching and stooping.

Frank patented the Gilbreth Platform and it came into widespread use. In his own construction business he increased its usefulness by placing one on each side of a wall, using two teams of bricklayers.

When Lillie began to work with him in the construction business she collaborated in a scheme which brought further efficiency and reduction of motion in bricklaying.

At a construction site bricks had always been loaded onto a wheelbarrow and dumped out by the side of the bricklayer. When the bricklayer picked up a brick he had to toss it several times to find its top and bottom, to determine if its edges had been chipped—and how best to lay it if they were, or whether to discard the brick if it had been chipped too badly.

In the Gilbreth scheme the bricks, all perfect, came to the bricklayer in a paper-covered package. The bricks were stacked uniformly. The bricklayer did not have to waste motions in tossing the bricks to find top and bottom. He did not have to examine them for chipped edges. He did not have to discard any. Chipped bricks which could be used in places where edges were not important came to the bricklayer in a different colored package.

The union wage for bricklayers at the time was $4.50 a day. Gilbreth was able to pay his men $6.50 a day because his system made them more productive.

Frank and Lillie Gilbreth explained the application of scientific management techniques and motion study to bricklaying in a book *Bricklaying System*. Today, a half century later, the book still is regarded as a classic in engineering circles.

The Gilbreths developed basic principles of scientific management which they asserted could, with adequate preparation, be applied in any plant. In various writings they told of these principles and Frank discussed them at engineering meetings.

Scientific management began to catch on in American industry. Manufacturers began to employ Frank to study their operations and reform them in accord with scientific principles. Lillie helped him in these undertakings.

At the same time a strong interest in the achievements and potentialities of the new science arose among the great mass of people, and book publishers and magazines urged the few experts in the field to write on it. At the request of one publisher Frank and Lillie Gilbreth wrote for popular reading *A Primer of Scientific Management*. However, authorship was credited only to Frank because the publisher believed that people would not buy a book on a technological subject coauthored by a woman.

Lillie again encountered prejudice against women when her book *The Psychology of Management* was published. At the publisher's insistence the author's name was given as L. M. Gilbreth and none of the publicity told that the author was a woman.

The Psychology of Management dealt with the synthesis

of psychological and managerial principles, and it was well received both in the United States and abroad. At professional meetings Frank sometimes would be asked if L. M. Gilbreth was related to him. He liked to reply, "Oh, just by marriage."

Frank's involvement in scientific management and motion study grew. Simultaneously his interest in construction dwindled, then ceased. This pleased Lillie. She had never cared much for construction; she took part in it because it was Frank's work. But scientific management with its promise of a better life for millions enthralled her. She was equally pleased for Frank's sake, believing that in the search for the one best way he would find his greatest satisfactions.

Manufacturers whose products were known throughout the world employed Frank to apply scientific management methods to their plants. A single job might take a year or more. He recruited and trained a force of technicians but Lillie was his most important aide, actually his junior partner.

Frank and his experts would spend weeks walking about a client plant, observing, talking with managers, foremen, and workers, making photographs. He would create a "process chart," showing the flow of raw materials to machines and their emergence as finished products, and study the chart for blocks, detours, and backtracking. He would make a scale model of the plant with tiny replicas of the machines, then shift the machines about to achieve the highest efficiency.

Under his direction a cameraman would make motion pictures of the workers at their jobs. Then Frank would run the films slowly and study them for needless motions, awkward motions, fatiguing motions. Later he would suggest new motions for each operation—easier ones, less tiring, more productive.

Lillie's contributions usually were in the psychological aspects of good management—morale, worker acceptance and participation, and education of the workers in new techniques.

The Gilbreths made it a practice to keep the workers informed of the purpose of their study and the recommendations it produced. This helped greatly to reduce the resistance which people often offer to things new and strange.

Motion study films were shown to the workers, who were invited to criticize their own techniques and techniques of co-workers, and to suggest improvements. Frequently some of the best ideas came from the workers themselves. Often the Gilbreths were able to induce plant owners to set up worker-management councils in which plant practices were criticized and proposals made and discussed for improvements. They favored trade unions as an aid to better labor-management relations and arbitration of labor-management disputes.

Frank and Lillie Gilbreth saw scientific management as industrial democracy, and they felt a job was successful when they were able to increase production while making work less arduous. They expected that employers who were enabled to cut costs by application of their methods would pass on a fair portion of the savings to the workers in higher wages.

Lillie oriented plant managers to the importance of proper selection and training of supervisory personnel. A brutal foreman, she would explain, could cause tension and psychological fatigue among his subordinates, rendering them more prone to accidents. And such a man, she would add, could cause an increase in absenteeism and resistance to work goals.

She indicated the types of personalities best suited for various jobs, and showed simple means of identifying these types.

One type of person, she instructed executives, detests tending a machine for the whole work day but does well in work involving movement and variety, while another type finds satisfaction in a repetitive task or the rhythmic pounding of a machine.

Decades ago Frank and Lillie Gilbreth put their stamp on the techniques, procedures, principles, and broadening democracy of modern industry.

They were living meanwhile a full and happy family life. Lillie bore twelve children in seventeen years. Child number seven, a girl, was given her name. Then came Fred, Dan, Jack, Bob, and Jane. Not all the children were to survive. Mary, the second oldest, died in her sixth year.

The Gilbreths settled in a comfortable fourteen-room house in Montclair, N.J. They spent their summers on Nantucket Island, off Cape Cod, where Frank bought a cottage. He named it The Shoe because such was the residence of the woman in the nursery rhyme who had so many children.

Aided by a cook and a handyman, Lillie ran the Montclair home. On its grounds were the business offices of Gilbreth, Inc., and a laboratory for experimentation in techniques of motion study.

Often Frank became so engrossed in the problems presented by a scientific management job that he spent on experimentation sums greatly exceeding his fee. There were periods when he was so preoccupied with experiments that he would not take on a job. He designed specialized equipment which cost thousands of dollars to construct.

To the children the house at 68 Eagle Rock Way, the offices, and the laboratory were all part of home. Frank and Lillie wanted it that way.

It was common for Frank to talk over a project with an engineer while several of the Gilbreth children sat taking notes, which would be discussed at dinner with their parents. When Frank went to look over a plant he often took two or three children with him. There were instances when he and Lillie took the whole family into a plant.

The household ran on principles of scientific management and cooperation. A Family Council of the parents and children established budgets, deciding how much should be spent for the children's clothing for the season, for entertainment and athletic equipment for the older children and toys for the younger ones. Such a matter as whether the family should acquire a dog also came before the Council.

The older children served on purchasing committees— one for clothing, a second for furniture and furnishings, and a third for groceries. The groceries committee, shopping around for the best deal, arranged with a distributor to buy canned goods at wholesale prices and these were delivered in truckload lots.

Excepting the current baby, each child had household assignments. Also each of the older children was responsible for a younger one. The older child had to help his charge get dressed and washed in the morning, make sure he put on clean clothes when he needed them, that he was on time for meals and carried out his chores. The older ones also tutored the younger ones if they were weak in a school subject and supervised their school homework.

All household chores were subject to constant study with the purpose of making them easier and quicker to accomplish. Frank took motion pictures of the children washing dishes and cutting the hedges and the whole family studied them.

Frank was the disciplinarian. Angered by misbehavior, he had a stern eye, a roaring voice, and a heavy hand. But his wife got better results with the children although she never spanked, threatened, or even raised her voice.

She saw her children as individuals, differing in personality, in emotional needs, in response to situations. When a child misbehaved she would talk it over with him. She might find that the child had struck a younger brother or sister to release anger caused by an incident in school, or ripped another's shirt because his own was a worn hand-me-down. She would try to deal with the real cause of the problem. She might explain that if he thought he had been treated unfairly by a teacher he should talk to the teacher about it; if he was unhappy about his worn shirt he should ask for another and not destroy a brother's or sister's garment.

A favorite activity of the family was to go for a ride in the Gilbreths' huge open touring car. Frank would drive and Lillie would also sit on the front seat, holding the baby, with one of the older children beside her. All the children wanted to sit with their parents and every few miles Frank would stop the car so the older children could rotate sitting in front.

In the wooded countryside they would stop the car and out would come thick sandwiches, fruit, and milk. The family would eat, then Frank in his bass and Lillie in her sweet soprano would lead the children in singing.

In this family every event was utilized for learning. Frank might seek out an ant hill and, with the children peering over his shoulder at the ants, would relate the work of the ants to engineering and industrial teamwork.

Lillie would make the children shiver with excitement with stories of nature. Finding a bird's nest, she would explain how wonderful was the instinct which impelled the mother bird to hatch and feed and protect her young. She would fish a pebble out of a stream and convey a sense of endless time by telling how the water had smoothed and rounded its sides over thousands of years.

In her forties, Lillie was little changed from the time she was a bride. Although she had borne twelve children she was as slim as a girl. She had never had a serious illness, and her eyes shone with happiness.

Frank, ten years older, had changed greatly. He had become quite stout and his heart was failing. He always carried a heart stimulant with him. Doctors told him he had not long to live, adding that if he stopped working he might prolong his life. He refused.

When the ailment was first detected in a medical examination the two youngest children had not yet been born. Frank suggested to Lillie that perhaps they shouldn't have any more children. He might die any day, he said, and each additional child would add to the burden she would have to carry.

Lillie said, "I don't think that eleven children would be any more trouble than nine. Besides, I like to finish what I start. Don't you?" He gazed at her as if nowhere in the world was there a woman like her.

Within three years she gave birth to Bob and Jane.

Early in June of 1924 Frank came home from a long trip to attend Ernestine's high school graduation and rest for a few days before sailing for Europe to take part in the World Power Conference and the International Management Conference. He was very tired. He had visited a number of industrial clients and given talks at the Universities of Michigan, Purdue, Harvard, Lehigh, and Columbia.

He slept late on the day after his daughter's graduation, then told Lillie he was going to take a commuter train to New York to have his passport stamped. Lillie walked with him from the door to the street where she picked some pieces of lint from his suit, ending with a pat on his chest. He grinned. "You always do that—the pat of finality."

His words were prophetic.

He telephoned her from the railroad station a short time later to say that he had forgotten his passport and wanted one of the children to bring it to him. Lillie told him to hold the line while she went to find the passport. When she picked up the telephone again there was no one on the line. Minutes later a white-faced neighbor came to tell her that she had been asked by the police to tell Mrs. Gilbreth that her husband had dropped dead.

Toward evening Frank's body was brought home and his wife and children sat with him, grieving. Soon a storm broke with a fury of wind, rain, and lightning.

Frank and Lillie had taught the children not to fear storms, as they had taught them that death was not fearful but rather a natural event of life. The storm held them spellbound and they watched it in silence until eleven-year-old William spoke.

"Isn't it just like Dad?" he asked, and the others agreed that its brilliance and power reminded them of their father.

Friends of Frank and Lillie Gilbreth feared she would be crushed by the tasks and responsibilities laid on her by his death. She was forty-six years old and all her life major decisions had been made for her, first by her parents, then Frank. There was little money, just Frank's insurance. She had eleven children, ranging from two-year-old Jane to Anne, who had just completed her sophomore year at Smith College. Just the cost of sending the children to college—forty-two years of college—was massive.

Moreover, her suffering was so intense that it pained her friends to look upon her face.

But they need not have feared. Responding to the greatest challenge of her life and to a trust left by a man she had loved without reserve, she grew in stature and determination. Suddenly she acquired a new decisiveness.

Two days after Frank's death Lillie convened the Family Council, sitting in his place as chairman. She told the children about the lack of money. Anne said she would leave college and get a job and others of the older children said they too would go to work. Lillie held up a hand. "Please let me finish," she said.

Lillie's mother—her father recently had died—had urged her to come with the children to California to live in the Moller home. Also, Lillie said, friends had offered to adopt some of the children or at least to pay for their education. Lillie said she had declined all offers.

"This is what I propose," she said, "and its success depends upon your being able to take over a lot more responsibility. Also it will involve your making sacrifices. So I want you to decide.

"I want us to remain together. I want each of you to go to college just as your father planned. I intend to go ahead with your father's work. I'll keep open the office and the laboratory. We'll continue to live in this house, but we'll have to sell the car and cut out everything we can do without. And you'll have to take care of each other more than ever before. Do you want to do it? If you do I'll take that boat your father was going to sail on and give those speeches for him in London and Prague. I'm sure that's the way he would have wanted it."

She looked about. Every head was nodding yes. A moment later the children scattered to help. Ernestine and Martha ran upstairs to pack Lillie's things. Anne went to the kitchen to plan dinner, and Frank and William walked down town to see about the sale of the car.

Lillie sailed for Europe with a contingent of engineers. To a friend on board the liner she said she felt no need for sympathy because "I have had more in twenty years of marriage than any other woman I have ever known has had in a lifetime."

She took part in the Power Conference in London, then traveled to Prague and attended the International Management Conference, presiding over one of the sessions in Frank's place. At each meeting she read a paper which she and Frank had prepared.

In Prague a memorial meeting was held for Frank and Lillie cried softly as speakers eulogized him as a great engineer and a great man, and one speaker said his motion

study contributions had "sweetened the work of every laborer."

Lillie was away five weeks. For this time her children,
who recently had lost their father, were deprived of their
mother whom they needed more than ever before in their
lives. It was a deprivation they bore with courage. The older
children knew the rightness of what their mother was doing
and the younger ones sensed it. They reacted by making the
fullest use of the strengths which were their heritage from a
home of love and emotional security, and their training in
work and cooperation.

Before leaving, Lillie had had time to make only one
economy move. She let the cook go, retaining Tom the
handyman. Tom liked to invent stories of his own heroism
and nothing he did came out quite right, but he had one
outstanding virtue—he loved the children. Lillie also left
$600 with Anne for the family's expenses.

Lillie was at sea en route to Europe when the first major
problem arose in the home. William came down with
chicken pox and quickly all the other children were infected. Anne, herself sick, handled the situation capably.

She had the family doctor look in on them all and assigned Tom to administer medication and cook the meals.
She had all the girls' beds moved into two rooms and the
boys' into two others adjacent to these. From her bed Anne
was able to see every child. She had each child get up long
enough to wash, remake his bed, and weigh himself.

Taught by her father to use all time for profit, she set up
a phonograph where it could be heard by the whole group
and played French and German recordings over and over
again so the children would absorb the foreign words and
sentence constructions.

In their daily letters to their mother the children never mentioned their illness and Lillie didn't learn of it until she came back to America.

After the children recovered from chicken pox they left for Nantucket and The Shoe, as Lillie had instructed. First, however, they cleaned the house at Montclair. The older children did the heavy work and dusted the high places; the younger ones ran for brooms and mops and dusted the lower parts of walls and the legs of tables.

The children also went over the family budget to see where savings could be made. They decided to economize on food by buying cheaper cuts of meat and eliminating steaks and roasts. They slashed the clothing allotment and reduced the fund for movies and other entertainment. William and Frank said it would be no sacrifice at all to give up going to dancing school. This was eliminated.

The children never had had liberal allowances. Now even these were cut by a system of fines. A child who left on the electric light or the cold water was fined two cents; hot water was four cents. Failure to do an assigned chore cost five cents.

When Lillie joined her children at The Shoe she found them healthily tanned, and they had saved $300.

Frank always believed that two colleges were better than one so in the fall Anne transferred from Smith to the University of Michigan. Sixteen-year-old Ernestine meanwhile entered Smith as a freshman.

Lillie set out to make a living in the profession she and Frank had helped develop. She let it be known in industry that she was available as a consultant in scientific management and motion study. At the same time she announced that, starting in early January of 1925, she would conduct at her home in Montclair a 16-week school in motion study for executives and college professors of management and engineering. She had helped Frank conduct four such schools, all successful.

That fall after Frank's death she worked for a Boston department store and a chain of laundries as a consultant, and did plant surveys at Rochester and Troy, New York. Some of this work was in fulfillment of contracts made by Frank. She made each trip away from home as brief as possible, speeding back to spend time with the nine children still at Montclair.

Tired and underweight, she made Thanksgiving dinner for her family but the chair which was Frank's seemed terribly empty. Two weeks later she fell ill with influenza and was in bed for three weeks.

Her doctor said she should rest after her illness but she was determined to go through with the school, which attracted three students. One came from a Providence asphalt company, the second from a firm manufacturing bandages and medical adhesive tape, and the third from Macy's Department Store in New York.

She worked again as a consultant in the spring, then began planning another school for the fall. She spent a month visiting industrial and merchandising executives to interest them in sending people to her school and another month working as a saleswoman in Macy's for first-hand experience in fatigue from the sales person's point of view. Her second school was successful. Several additional large stores, industries and the Sears Roebuck mail-order firm were represented.

She conducted five more schools and each was more successful than the last. Students came to her from Belgium, Germany, Great Britain, France, Czechoslovakia, and Japan.

The first half dozen years after Frank died were years of great difficulty for her. It seemed to her that the pain of losing him would never soften. She struggled to meet the financial needs of her family. She borrowed from her mother to get out of one crisis and met another by asking her third daughter, Martha, to postpone going to college for a year. But all the time her reputation was growing and the job offers were becoming more numerous.

Her nerves were taut. When Anne came home for vacation from college and burst out that she had fallen in love with a young doctor Lillie wept. In the strain under which she was living, the first meaning of Anne's announcement was that she was losing her child. Later Lillie made it plain to Anne that she was truly happy.

Away from home, she worried over what might happen to the children. Once a niece met Lillie at the railroad station in Montclair with the greeting, "I have news for you." Lillie turned white. Then when it turned out that the news was that Anne had been elected to Phi Beta Kappa, the college honor society, she sat down on the curbstone and wept in relief.

But as a mother and as an engineer evidence of her success multiplied. Her children were healthy and happy. Each year one of them graduated from high school or college. Then they married and Lillie Gilbreth learned the happiness of being a grandmother.

Her reputation grew greater and reached into foreign countries. Great industries sought her services.

She was just emerging from her economic difficulties when the great depression struck in 1929. With industry seeking greater efficiency and means of cutting waste, the demand for her skills rose sharply. But when the next year President Herbert Hoover asked her to head the woman's division of the President's Emergency Committee for Employment, she canceled every engagement and went to Washington.

Under her direction leaders in thousands of women's clubs throughout the country took on responsibility for job surveys which would show how those with funds could utilize the services of the unemployed at fair rates of pay. Within a few weeks the Share the Work Plan was bearing results. Arthur Woods, Chairman of the Emergency Committee, said, "Dr. Gilbreth conceived a new method to apply to an old evil . . . a brilliant conception carried through with speed and skill."

Later she served on the President's Organization on Unemployment Relief. In this position she attempted to draw the attention of government and industrial leaders to the need for better planning to avoid depressions and waste of America's human and material resources.

Her work for the nation done, she went back to serving industry. She lectured at universities and counseled foreign governments. She wrote extensively, in time more than a score of books.

For a time she served as Professor of Management at Purdue University School of Engineering, the first woman to hold such a post. Then she served as Chairman of the Department of Personnel Relations at the Newark College of Engineering, again pioneering as a woman in such a position.

Throughout the world people began to speak of shy, humble Lillie Gilbreth as "the world's greatest woman engineer" and "the first lady of engineering." Universities gave her honorary degrees, Michigan, alma mater of Anne, Frank, and Jane; Smith, the college of Ernestine and young Lillian; Rutgers, Martha's school; Purdue, William's school; Brown, Fred's—more than a dozen in all.

When World War Two came she saw five of her six sons go off to fight while the sixth was turned back because of a heart ailment. She went to work for the War Manpower Board and perhaps no other person did more to integrate American women into the defense effort. She was over sixty and her hair was white. But her body was slender and erect. She worked sixty, seventy, and eighty hours a week for her country.

She used her skills and knowledge of motion study to aid the rehabilitation of men handicapped by wounds. She designed special training methods for the handicapped and went about the country explaining them to industrialists and business executives. As she traveled she found great satisfaction in seeing people she had trained—a number of them women—in positions of responsibility.

Honors came to her. She never sought them and she accepted them with humbleness. In 1941 the General Federation of Women's Clubs selected her as one of fifty-three women whose work typified the great advance made by women in the preceding half century. In 1948 she was named Woman of the Year by the American Women's Association.

She was given the Washington Award, "an honor conferred upon an engineer by fellow-engineers for accomplishments which preeminently promote the happiness, comfort, and well-being of humanity." Previous recipients included Herbert Hoover; Orville Wright, inventor of the airplane; and Henry Ford.

The National Institute of Social Sciences gave her its Gold Medal for "distinguished service to humanity."

She turned seventy, working still, a straight-backed woman with alert, calm eyes. Nearing eighty, she was working yet, giving priority to two causes, the training of young people and the rehabilitation of the handicapped.

In the manner of the Gilbreth system she utilized every hour for advantage. In her seventy-ninth year she was invited to take part in a one-day engineering conference in Mexico. She accepted but allotted it just one working day, although it involved traveling there from New York and returning. The night before the conference opened she spent flying to Mexico, sleeping. And when the conference was over she embarked for home, sleeping again. She arrived in New York in the morning and resumed work.

Within one period of six months she worked, mainly training young engineers, in the Philippines, Formosa, and India.

Each year she managed to see every member of her family, residing along both coasts of the United States and in places in between. There were now besides the eleven children and their spouses, twenty-eight grandchildren—three married—and one great-grandson.

She did this in the course of her work, making side trips from cities where her work took her. Also each of her children and their spouses and the older grandchildren had a key to her apartment in Montclair. Often when she came home from a trip she would find one or two making a sandwich, stretched out on a sofa reading or asleep in bed.

The Family Council still functioned. "If one member has a problem on which he wants to be advised," she said, "he consults with members of the family living nearest him or who are specially equipped to deal with his problem. If it's something very important the whole Family Council will get together.

"I'm just one member of the Council." She said it proudly. The achievements of Dr. Lillian M. Gilbreth gave her no special status in the family democracy. And her remark measured the success of Lillie and Frank Gilbreth as parents.

She sat in the headquarters of the Society of Mechanical Engineers in New York on a summer day. She had just returned from the University of Connecticut where she had helped make a film to aid handicapped mothers with pre-school children. Soon she would leave for other states and for Europe, to work.

"Do you ever think of retiring?" she was asked.

"I am retired," she said and smiled a little at her reply. "When my children were young I had to provide for them and it was a struggle. Sometimes I took on jobs I didn't like much, for people I didn't admire. Now my children are grown, they don't need me. I have to provide only for myself, and my needs are simple.

"So I do only what I really want to do—I think of this as retirement, doing just what you want to do."

Amelia Earhart

Poised at the start of the 3,000-foot runway, the big silver plane throbbed with the roar of its two engines. By the control tower some thirty natives, naked to the waist, grinned and covered their ears.

These villagers who lived near the airport hacked out of the jungle at Lae, New Guinea, were used to airplanes, for the Guinea Airways Company made heavy use of the field in flying passengers and mining equipment to the gold fields in the interior.

But they had never seen a woman piloting a plane, not even one of the *nutungs*—insects—their term for a small aircraft. The slim yellow-haired woman at the controls made it exciting. They understood only dimly the incredible distance the plane was going to try to fly. But the handful of white onlookers knew, and the natives sensed their awe and tension.

The signal went out from the control tower. The woman in the cockpit touched her hand to her head in a salute, and the plane lurched and then taxied down the runway.

Burdened with more than 1,000 gallons of gasoline and oil, the plane seemed unable to free itself from the runway, ending abruptly on a cliff overhanging the ocean. When it seemed to the onlookers too late to avoid disaster, the straining aircraft lifted from the ground and skimmed out over the water.

Exactly one month before, June 1, 1937, Amelia Earhart and her navigator, Fred Noonan, had started on a flight around the world, a distance of 29,000 miles. Such a flight had never before been accomplished. Six years before, Wiley Post, later killed with the humorist Will Rogers when their monoplane crashed in Alaska, had made the first round-the-world flight. But his route was around the top of the world—some 15,500 miles.

From the time she kissed her husband good-by at the Municipal Airport in Miami, Florida, and flew into the sunrise, an eager world had followed the flight of the First Lady of Aviation.

From the strange and colorful places on the globe where she set down for the plane's and crew's essential four R's— refueling, repairs, refreshment, and rest—came the news dispatches which fed the interest of millions.

San Juan, Puerto Rico. Caripito, Venezuela, with its huge oil tanks on the perimeter of the airport menacing incoming planes. Zandery airfield serving the Dutch Guiana capital of Paramaribo. A hop of 350 miles over ocean and 1,000 more over jungle to Fortaleza, Brazil. A two-hour flight to Natal, Brazil. Then a takeoff in predawn darkness and across the Atlantic to St. Louis on the coast of Africa. Khartoum in the Sudan. Assab on the Red Sea. Karachi, due to become the capital of Pakistan.

At Karachi a newspaperwoman asked her how far she had already flown. Amelia figured it out. "About 15,000 miles—about 100 hours in the air," she said.

The flight continued. Calcutta and a difficult landing in a dust storm. Across India in a monsoon which whipped up a wind so savage it wore the paint off the edges of the wings. Rangoon. Singapore. Bandung in Java. Port Darwin on the north coast of Australia.

Lae, New Guinea, and the plane rested on the shore of the Pacific. The parachutes carried since Miami had been dropped off at Port Darwin. Of what use would they be over the great lonely ocean? Twenty-two thousand miles had been recorded on the log. Ahead, seven thousand miles away, lay California.

Now the longest and most dangerous leg of the journey —2,550 miles across the water to Howland Island, a speck on the map near the equator.

Near Howland the Coast Guard cutter *Itasca* was stationed, waiting to guide the plane in. After midnight on July 2 officers and men crowded into the radio room of the cutter waiting to hear Amelia Earhart's first signal.

At 2:45 A.M. the radio operator waved his hand for silence. He had picked up a broadcast. But the message was garbled, he said.

An hour later he picked up another, asking for a directional broadcast. He sent one out.

"She'll be in by dawn," he said confidently.

Dawn came and the Coast Guardsmen on the deck searched the sky. It was empty.

At 7:30 A.M. another message came. It brought fear aboard the cutter.

"We must be on you, but cannot get you. Gas is running low . . . We are flying at 1,000 feet. . . ."

Every avaliable man was ordered to the deck, told to

strain his eyes and ears. The radio operator broadcast directional signals. Over and over.

At 7:57 her voice was heard once more.

"We are circling but cannot see the island . . . cannot hear you . . ."

Nothing more. Silence.

While the world heard of her disappearance with shock, a giant sea and air search unfolded. The *Itasca* began alone. Freighters hundreds of miles from the flight route turned from course to enter the search. The mine sweeper *Swan* joined them.

Three days after Amelia Earhart disappeared, the battleship *Colorado*, carrying three planes, arrived at Howland from Honolulu. A week later an aircraft carrier with a full compliment of planes and escorted by four destroyers steamed in from San Diego, California.

Ships and planes covered thousands of miles, over and over again. No trace of the silver plane was ever found.

Amelia Earhart used to say to her husband, George Palmer Putnam, "When I go, I'd like best to go in my plane. Quickly."

Most people who met Amelia Earhart for the first time were surprised. They thought that a woman who flew large planes incredible distances at incredible speeds would be mannish and unattractive.

Instead they saw a woman utterly feminine and lovely—and when not in flying clothes, she was pleasingly dressed, sometimes in gowns of her own design.

Usually they noticed her hands—long, slender, beautiful. The hands of a pianist. They were often painted and sculptured by artists.

There were other surprising things about her. Beginning with the time that she first flew the Atlantic, millions of words were written about her. She rarely read them. After she had performed some outstanding feat in the air someone would invariably say, naming a newspaper or magazine, "Have you read the wonderful article about you in the ——?" Usually she would answer, "No, I haven't. I know I did it and how I did it and all the things that happened. Why do I have to read about it?"

She cared little for honors. Governments and kings and eminent scientific organizations awarded her gold medals and jeweled decorations. She kept them in a little suitcase; the suitcase she kept in a bedroom drawer. None of her friends ever saw them.

Some people found it hard to square her indifference to honors with her challenges of time and distance in the air, which won her more honors. "Why do you do it?" she used to be asked. "Why do you fly?"

Her usual answer was, "Because I want to."

She was criticized for that. It seemed a frivolous reason.

But it wasn't frivolous at all. For when, sometimes, she spoke more fully it became plain that her purpose was a mature and idealistic one. She said: "This isn't a reason to be apologized for. It is the most honest motive of mankind's achievements.

"To want in one's heart to do a thing for its own sake; to enjoy doing it; to concentrate one's energies upon it— that is not only the surest guarantee of its success, it is also being true to one's self."

All the thirty-nine years that she lived Amelia Earhart was true to herself. She did what her heart prompted—

even if people disapproved. But always she acted out her freedom with regard for others.

She was born in Atchison, Kansas, in 1898. Her father was a lawyer. He was handsome and brilliant. But he was not a successful man. It is likely that he wasn't even interested in success. He made a modest living doing law work for railroads.

People in Atchison said that Mr. Earhart was somewhat unconventional. A case in point was his love of fishing. People in this conservative community could understand that. But they couldn't understand why Mr. Earhart insisted on doing most of his fishing on Sundays. That caused talk.

When Amelia and her sister Muriel were little girls he used to explain with a twinkle in his eye, "It's a proven fact that the fish bite best on Sundays." Actually, he did it because in his boyhood he was punished severely for fishing on Sunday; and he vowed that when he was a man he would do as he liked about it.

He taught his two girls the pleasure of fishing and the three of them were often seen walking to the river carrying bamboo poles and cans of worms.

How the tongues wagged at the sight, for it was evident that Mrs. Earhart also was somewhat odd. She dressed her two little girls in boys' blue jeans. This in the early 1900's!

Amelia and Muriel could throw a baseball as far and straight as a boy. Their father taught them. No reason why girls shouldn't enjoy games as much as boys, he said.

In those days girls went sledding in the winter on high-sided sleds with wooden runners, sitting erect like little ladies. Mr. Earhart jeered at that. He bought for Amelia and Muriel boys' sleds, built close to the ground and with steel runners, and showed them how to coast on their stomachs with a running belly-bump start.

Years later Amelia often spoke out against the philosophy that girls should be prepared for "women's work" and boys for "men's work."

Girls, she said, should be encouraged and enabled to take up any work they wanted and were qualified for. She asked what good reason is there for not teaching girls how to use a hammer and saw, how to stop a faucet leak or paint a fence?

Boys, she said, should learn about shopping for the household and nutrition, should know how to cook, how to diaper an infant. "Otherwise they are inadequately prepared for marriage," she said.

In her childhood her mother taught her cooking and sewing; her father, the use of tools. Once she and Muriel constructed their own version of a roller coaster they had seen at a fair, an incline from the roof of the barn to the ground made of old boards; the vehicle, a wooden platform on old roller skate wheels.

In the Earhart home reading was much encouraged, as well as an interest in the wonders of the world and the universe. At six Amelia was permitted to stay up until nearly midnight to see an eclipse of the moon, which her father explained to her.

She and Muriel kept frogs, lizards, and harmless snakes, collected spiders and rare moths.

Amelia's teachers said she was a bright child, eager to try anything new, intensely curious about things she didn't understand. She was not shy, they said, not insecure—but she was never part of the group. She seemed to prefer being alone.

Her teachers remarked on a curious trait of the lean tow-headed youngster. She was always near the head of the class and with a little more effort could have won prizes, but she never cared to. One teacher said, "She seemed satisfied just to know that she could win if she wanted to."

The nature of Mr. Earhart's railroad law work changed when Amelia came into her teens. He had to move about a good deal, six months in this city, nine months or a year in that. His family went with him.

This gypsylike rootlessness does not seem to have done any harm to Amelia's personality. Rather she developed a faculty for quick adjustment to a strange environment, for feeling comfortable among new people. Those who knew her in her high school years said she was a friendly girl with an unusual natural poise for her age.

At seventeen she was graduated from Hyde Park High School in Chicago. It was the sixth high school she had attended in four years. Then Amelia went off to a private school for girls in Philadelphia and Muriel to college in Toronto.

Amelia had at this time no set idea of what she wanted to do. This wasn't for lack of ambitions. She had many—practicing medicine, being a physicist, teaching, doing social work, to name a few. There were so many useful and gratifying things she would like to do. She had a notion that she might spend a few years at each.

The notion of adolescence became the philosophy of maturity. In her early thirties she observed with satisfaction that she already had had twenty-eight different jobs and hoped to have scores more. She was always looking for better things to do. But while she looked she performed the task at hand with energy and enthusiasm.

In her third year at the Philadelphia school she abruptly gave up her studies because she saw a job that urgently needed doing.

She was spending the Christmas vacation of 1917 with Muriel in Toronto. It was the third year of World War One. Canada had been in the war since its beginning.

Amelia had followed the conflict in the newspapers and was saddened by its cost in casualties and suffering. On Toronto's King Street, the sight of four ex-soldiers on crutches, each with an empty trouser leg, shocked her into a deeper understanding of the suffering caused by war.

To return to school seemed an evasion of a responsibility to the wounded. She went to the Spadina Military Hospital in Toronto and became a nurse's aide without pay.

For the next year she bathed and fed wounded men sent home from the front to recuperate, renewed dressings, changed bed linen and pushed the disabled in wheel chairs.

On one of her days off she went with another girl to the Toronto Fair Grounds to see a flying exhibition by a Canadian war ace returned from combat in Europe.

It was only fifteen years since Wilbur and Orville Wright had made the world's first power-driven flight in a rickety little plane of their own invention. Airplanes were still so rare that people craned their necks to look whenever one flew overhead. Most people thought of them as quite remote from their lives.

In this respect Amelia was one of the majority. She had no particular interest in the airplane.

At the Fair Grounds she saw one at close range for the first time, before the pilot took it up. She saw the pilot not as a distant doll-size head in helmet and goggles rising from the cockpit but as a full-size human with recognizable and individual features.

Then this flier, this distinctly individual man—the things he did with his plane! He looped, spun and dived. She held her breath. Her face became moist with perspiration.

She stood with her friend apart from the other onlookers. From 2,500 feet, directly above the girls, the pilot put his plane into a power dive. Her friend ran, but Amelia stood fascinated. Her fears painted a dreadful picture of what would happen if the pilot could not pull out of the dive. But she felt such a pleasure at the sight of the plane roaring down, becoming larger, that she was held spellbound.

She came away from the exhibition in a state of happy excitement.

Henceforth there was a realness about the planes she saw in the sky, and articles about aviation in newspapers and magazines drew her attention.

As the time came for her to leave the military hospital she decided to study medicine. She enrolled at Columbia University in New York for a premedical course. Feeling that this would not give her an education quickly enough, she also enrolled at Barnard College. For a year she studied at both schools—and did well.

Her father, meanwhile, had become ill and retired from work. He and Mrs. Earhart had moved to California, near Los Angeles. After a year at college Amelia left New York to join them.

Soon her interest in aviation became active. She visited

the primitive airfields of the day and attended air meets. Visiting one "airfield," a few acres of scrubby ground with a shed containing drums of gasoline, she decided to go aloft. Her pilot was Frank Hawks, who later became one of America's best known fliers, establishing more than two hundred records in a two-year period.

At supper her father and mother questioned her about how it felt. Was she nervous? Frightened? What did she think about in the air?

"I felt," she said, "as if I were among friends."

She ate in silence for a minute. Then she said matter-of-factly, "I think I'll learn to fly."

"Good," Mr. Earhart said. "When do you begin?"

He was joking because he thought she was. But Amelia was in earnest.

Lessons, she learned, would cost about $1,000. She got a clerical job with the telephone company in Los Angeles and paid for the lessons with her earnings. These weren't very big and she begrudged spending money for lunches and clothes. But one garment she deemed essential—a flying coat.

It cost $20 at a sale and was of patent leather. But when she wore it for the first time at the little airfield where she took her lessons she felt conspicuous. The leather coats of the experienced fliers were wrinkled, dulled and stained. Hers was new and shiny.

It was summer and it was hot, but she slept in the coat for three nights to wrinkle it. Then she rubbed the gloss off with a piece of rough cloth.

The wonderful day came when she was ready to solo. She took a little biplane—a Kinner Airster, it was called—up to 5,000 feet, flew out over the shore line, flew back over the airfield and idled about for a time. Then she came down in a good landing.

She felt, she said, such a deep happiness, a mood so intensely personal, that she was too embarrassed to tell about it.

With Mrs. Earhart's financial help Amelia bought a small second-hand plane and she spent every hour she could flying or talking shop at the field.

She decided one day to see how high she could go and climbed to 14,000 feet in her open cockpit plane with a three-cylinder engine. At the time it was a new altitude record for women. Of course, few women were flying then.

A week or two later she made an effort to go higher. She climbed to 11,000 feet and flew into a cloud bank and wind-driven snow which coated her goggles. She tried to fly out of the bank by climbing but found only heavy fog and sleet.

She was assailed by her first strong fear in the air. She could not see, not even her wings. Was one wing dipping? Was the plane turning? It was impossible to tell. The impulse to see the ground, to touch it, possessed her. She had to go down the quickest way. She put the plane into a spin. It seemed it would never end though actually it took less than a minute to drop below the fog and clouds and bring the green earth into view.

On the ground a mechanic asked her, "Why the spin?"

"I got frightened in the clouds," she said. "Spinning seemed the fastest way to get down."

"Get smart," the man said. "Suppose the fog was all the way to the ground. We'd be picking up the pieces now."

"Thank you," she said. "I'll know better next time."

Once she had left her premedical education, Amelia decided she did not want to become a doctor. In California she worked at several jobs, none very meaningful to her. At 26 she made up her mind to prepare herself for work that would be both gratifying and challenging, like social work or teaching.

She attended Harvard summer school in 1925 and then looked for a job as a social worker with Denison House, a settlement house in an immigrant section of Boston. There was no opening so she took a job teaching English for the Massachusetts University Extension. In 1927 an opening materialized at Denison House, and she went there to live as a member of the resident staff.

She directed the kindergarten and the activities of girls from six to fourteen. The forty or fifty girls in her charge were Chinese, Syrian, Armenian, Italian, Greek and Russian.

The purpose of social work she envisioned as "more to prevent failures in adjustment to living than to cure them."

She taught girls with mutual racial antagonisms inherent in old-country cultures to work and play together and form friendships. She made her girls aware of their latent talents and encouraged their development.

Many times she visited immigrant parents to plead that they sacrifice—and often it was a painful sacrifice—to keep a promising child in school.

On weekends, meanwhile, she borrowed a plane and flew over Boston and short distances north and south along the Atlantic shore. She became well known among Boston's small company of fliers. She joined the Boston chapter of the National Aeronautic Association and was elected vice president.

A picture of Amelia Earhart about to turn thirty shows

a slender young woman with hair cut boyishly short and steady eyes with a hint of reserve. A likable face, a face with beauty and strength.

It was a picture only a few people could have put a name to. Then, starting with a telephone call, an event of great drama occurred which transformed an obscure social worker and part-time flier into an international figure with a name and face known to hundreds of millions.

It was a weekday afternoon. At Denison House she was trying to bring to order some thirty girls whose natural exuberance had been suppressed by six hours of discipline in a nearby school.

A member of the staff caught Amelia's eye and gestured as if she were holding a telephone to her ear, shouting, "Call for you."

Amelia held her arms wide in resignation, as if to say, "How can I leave now?" The other woman shouted, "He says it's important."

Amelia excused herself and went to the phone. A man's voice said, "Miss Earhart? My name is Captain Hilton Railey. Would you be interested in doing something important in the air—but dangerous?"

She was silent. Prohibition was the federal law. Several times mysterious men had telephoned her with offers of rich rewards if she would fly whiskey into the United States from Canada. Was this another such proposition?

Captain Railey asked, "Miss Earhart, are you there? Do you hear me?" He suggested that they meet that evening so he could explain. She asked for references and he supplied them, the names of people well known in Boston. She said she would call these people and if they vouched for Captain Railey she would meet him.

The people she called said Captain Railey was of excellent reputation, and a gentleman.

Her thoughts for the remainder of the afternoon were about the meeting. What would Captain Railey propose? Testing a new plane? A scientific experiment in the air? An aerial exhibition of some kind?

He did not keep her long in suspense when they met. "Miss Earhart, would you like to fly the Atlantic?" he asked.

She thought only seconds. "Yes," she said. "Yes, with a good plane and an experienced crew."

Captain Railey explained that he had sounded her out in behalf of others. Now it was necessary that she be interviewed by these others, in New York.

She went to New York a few days later and there was informed of the background of the projected Atlantic flight. Mrs. Frederick Guest, a woman of social position and considerable financial means, had made up her mind to fly the Atlantic to dramatize the advancement of women. She purchased a plane, and began to search for a crew. But Mrs. Guest's family objected so strenuously that she decided against making the flight herself.

She commissioned George Palmer Putnam to find another American woman to go in her place. Putnam, a publisher and promoter, enlisted friends in various cities to look for candidates. One of these friends was Railey, who approached Amelia.

In this way Amelia came to meet the man she was to marry. Putnam, tall, wearing glasses, interviewed her in New York. She showed her pilot's license from the Federation Aeronautique Internationale, the first granted an American woman. She had qualified for the license while she was in California.

Putnam asked her questions, encouraged her to talk—
about flying, her work at Denison House, her education.
Meanwhile he watched her carefully.

There were certain requirements the candidate had to
meet, he said with a smile. In addition to being a flier, she
needed to have intelligence, education, grace, and charm.
She also had to be attractive.

So far as he was concerned, Putnam said, Amelia met the
requirements. The next thing she had to do, he said, was
have an interview with two other men associated with him
in selecting a woman for the flight.

She met the men and had much the same kind of talk as
with Putnam.

Several days later in Boston Amelia got a call from the
publisher. He told her she had been chosen to fly the Atlantic as one of a three-member crew. Her longest flight
until now had been about fifty miles.

Today aerial highways crisscross the Atlantic, connecting
terminals in North and South America with those in Europe
and Africa. On them thousands of passengers and thousands
of tons of freight are carried every year.

In 1928 the air over the Atlantic was empty. It was only
a year since the first nonstop flight had been made over the
Atlantic, by a lanky air mail pilot who landed in Paris and
announced, "I am Charles Lindbergh of the United States."

There were no radio beams for a plane to follow across
the ocean in 1928, no radio communications with airports
if anything went wrong, no broadcasts of weather and
flight conditions ahead.

And the plane, a Fokker, which Amelia was to fly was of
puny power and fragile construction compared to the sleek
giants which fly high over the seas today.

Plans for the flight, to originate in Boston, were kept secret. Putnam felt there would be greater dramatic impact in an announcement after the Fokker, named *Friendship*, was airborne.

Pontoons purchased from polar explorer Richard Byrd were attached to the plane. Bill Stultz, the pilot, and Lou Gordon, the mechanic, carefully overhauled the plane and tested it in the air.

Those who saw the preparations going on surmised that Byrd was going to use the plane in his forthcoming Antarctic expedition. Putnam, who came to Boston to oversee the preparations, did not correct their misapprehensions.

He instructed Amelia to stay away from the *Friendship* because she was well known in Boston air circles and people might start asking questions.

Amelia told only her superior at Denison House; and she continued working there. Meanwhile she and Putnam got to know each other better. They visited the Boston Public Gardens and fed peanuts to the pigeons. He took her to dinner. Several times he took her to visit Byrd and his wife Marie at their home on Brimmer Street where supplies and equipment for polar exploration, from tins of dried beef to ice axes, were piled to the ceiling in almost every room.

Friends of Byrd, airmen and fellow explorers, were usually at his home when Putnam and Amelia called. They told stories of their expeditions and Amelia's eyes shone with excitement as she listened. Putnam listened too, and watched her. A very lovely young woman, he mused.

The preparations finished, the fliers waited three weeks for favorable weather conditions. Then before dawn on a Sunday in late May they were ferried by a tugboat across Boston Harbor to where the plane was moored. Stultz warmed up the motors and the *Friendship* drove downwind, the pontoons slapping the waves furiously. When the speed reached sixty miles an hour the plane lifted off the water and began a slow climb.

The yellow-winged Fokker was hardly a hundred miles offshore when radio stations began interrupting scheduled programs with bulletin announcements that a young woman was flying the Atlantic. The afternoon newspapers carried the story in greater detail under large headlines.

More radio bulletins and newspaper stories publicized the plane's scheduled landing in the finger-like harbor of Trepassey, a fishing village on Newfoundland's southern shore.

Fog and adverse winds grounded the fliers at Trepassey for two weeks of boredom and impatience and a diet of rabbit, fish, and mutton.

A morning came when conditions were "reasonably good" and the *Friendship* took off again, pointing her nose eastward to the British Isles 2,000 miles away.

It had been planned that Amelia would take over the controls for part of the journey as a copilot, but shortly after the plane left Trepassey it ran into clouds and haze which persisted almost all the way across the ocean. Under these conditions Amelia thought it wisest for Stultz, a much more experienced pilot, to stay at the controls.

Throughout the day and night Amelia crouched in the tiny cabin or sat wedged between the gasoline tanks in the fuselage. In the morning, when the crew had been aloft nearly nineteen hours, the mechanic Gordon thrust a measuring stick in the gas tanks and shook his head doubtfully. "About two hours left," he said.

Amelia peered fixedly through the window, looking for

land. Several times her heart gave a jump; she was sure she saw land. But in each instance it was a mirage.

Shortly after Gordon measured the fuel again—and said there was only enough for an hour's flying—the fliers sighted a liner which they later learned was the *America*. Their radio had stopped working and they had to get their bearings. Stultz circled low over the liner and Amelia hastily wrote a note asking the ship to paint a bearing on the deck.

With a piece of cord she tied an orange to the note to give it more weight and dropped it, aiming for the deck. Note and orange fell in the sea and passengers on the liner merely waved.

About five minutes' supply of gas had been consumed in the detour. Stultz went back to his course and the three in the plane resumed their lookout for land.

Fifteen miles along they saw several small craft in the sea and the thought came to each: such little ships had to be near land. Then a smudge of gray showed on the horizon. It wasn't a mirage because it didn't disappear but grew larger. It was land!

Stultz guided the plane above a coastline, found a sheltered inlet and brought the Fokker down offshore from a village. The village was Burry Port, Wales.

A policeman rowed out to the plane and brought the fliers to shore. Exhausted, they went to sleep. Meanwhile telegraph wires and cables hummed with the news that a woman had flown the Atlantic for the first time.

The fliers refueled the next day and flew on to Southampton, Amelia handling the plane. She was besieged by reporters. They went on to London by motor car and more reporters descended upon her. Then followed a shower of congratulatory cables, telegrams, and letters.

President Calvin Coolidge was among those who cabled congratulations to "the first woman to fly the Atlantic." She replied to the President that "the success was entirely due to the great skill of Mr. Stultz."

But, as the reporters made clear, it was her the world was interested in. They wanted to know everything she did over the Atlantic. She protested that "the bravest thing I did myself was to try to drop an orange and a note on the head of an ocean liner captain—and I missed the whole ship." But she couldn't shunt aside their interest in her.

The great men of England invited her to dinners and receptions. It had never occurred to her that this would happen. All the wardrobe she had consisted of the bulky flying suit and the high laced boots she had worn on the plane.

She stayed at the London house of Mrs. Guest, who had financed the flight, and hastily purchased suitable clothes for the numerous appearances she was called on to make.

One evening following a military pageant she was feted at a party at an exclusive London club. An equerry came to her table and whispered that His Royal Highness the Prince of Wales was sitting nearby and asked the pleasure of a dance with her.

They danced—the tall, lovely American girl and the handsome prince who was later to reign so briefly.

The *Friendship* was sold in England, and Amelia went home by boat. This gave her a better idea of how much water she had flown over.

America opened its arms to the slim young woman flier. In New York she was given a tremendous reception and a ticker-tape parade ending at City Hall where a medal was conferred on her. She went to Boston and Chicago where she was given medals. Thirty-two other cities invited her to take part in local ceremonies honoring her.

The acclaim wasn't something she enjoyed particularly. She felt that it should go to Stultz and Gordon. "As women achieve more," she told friends, "this sort of special attention will diminish."

At the suggestion of Putnam, she accepted three invitations. Then she took a vacation. She flew across the country to California and back in leisurely hops of a few hundred miles, landing each day at dark.

In a serialized story of her life published while she was vacationing Amelia was described as "a girl who has everything—youth, intelligence, beauty, personality, and a promising future." The writer could not know of course that Amelia's future had a nine-year limit.

There was such a short time left to her. But in it she packed a prodigious measure of living and doing, and happiness and satisfaction.

At the outset she had a siege of offers—of generous fees to endorse products, of speaking engagements, of jobs. Even of marriage, which astonished her.

Putnam became her adviser, and together they sifted the offers. But it was she who made the decisions, in accord with her values and basic interests—in people, in the progress of women, in aviation.

She became aviation editor of a magazine of mass circulation "because it gave me a chance to reach a great many people with my special interest, aviation." She wrote articles and answered letters—by the hundreds—about all aspects of flying.

It pleased her that many of the letters were from young

people seeking to enter aviation, and from the parents of these youngsters. She was impressed with the serious thinking which many of the young people had obviously given to their future. But now and then a letter caused her to chuckle. Like the one from a young man who wrote: "Dear Miss Earhart: I have had a fight with my girl friend. I want to take up flying. Please tell me how."

Commercial airlines were struggling to establish themselves. While doing her magazine work Amelia also took on a job for one of the lines. Her function was to convince women of the comfort and advantages of flying. She traveled about in her own plane, addressing conventions of women's social and professional organizations.

On many of these trips her mother went with her. Mrs. Earhart got to feel so comfortable and relaxed in the air, that she always took a book along on long trips so she wouldn't fall asleep.

Amelia, meanwhile, was becoming highly skilled as a pilot and accumulating knowledge through her flights and talks with airmen, plane designers, and manufacturers.

She was one of the first to fly an autogiro, a relative of the present-day helicopter, taking one across the country to demonstrate its durability. At the invitation of the manufacturer she also took one up in an altitude test to determine how high it would fly.

In those days a pilot who flew above 16,000 feet risked blacking out from lack of oxygen. The mechanism which pumped a smooth flow of oxygen to pilots was still in the future. Amelia ascended with a primitive substitute, a bottle of oxygen from which she would inhale if she felt faint or dizzy. She took the autogiro up to 18,415 feet and didn't need the oxygen. The only discomfort she felt was from extreme cold in the open cockpit.

She gave numerous talks urging women to go into aviation in all its branches. In one talk in the fall of 1931 she reported that there were 472 women licensed pilots in the United States, more than in all the rest of the world, compared with twelve two years earlier.

Sometimes she told anecdotes of women who were combining careers in aviation with marriage, women who were mothers and even grandmothers. But she resisted marriage for herself.

George Putnam had proposed to her. She loved him. But she wouldn't marry him. Marriage, she said worriedly, was permanent, a commitment for life. She hated to contract for anything for life. She needed to be free to do what she liked. Marriage carried obligations which impinged on freedom. And then there was her occasional but intense need for solitude. Single, she didn't have to think of anyone else when she wanted to get away somewhere.

Putnam was patient and reasoning. He talked with Amelia about her needs and feelings about marriage. Their marriage need not imply obligation, he said. What they would give to each other would be entirely voluntary. Each would respect the other's needs. Marriage, Putnam pointed out, did not have to be a taking away of something; rather, it could mean a gaining of love and companionship.

With some uncertainty she said "yes." They were married in February, 1931, at the home of Putnam's mother in Connecticut.

Her fears of marriage were unjustified. Marriage brought her and Putnam great happiness. They settled in a house in Rye, New York, which became a home of warmth and contentment. She did her job—or rather jobs—hopping about the country. Putnam did his work. But many months of the year they spent together at home.

Amelia took up gardening and was pleased when her husband or guests praised her home-grown vegetables. She and Putnam enjoyed music together, reading to each other— she loved poetry—a canter along a woodland path, a swim in Long Island Sound nearby.

They entertained friends on evenings and weekends devoted to fellowship and good conversation. Amelia didn't like housework and day-to-day cooking but sometimes when guests came she went into the kitchen and prepared a strange foreign dish.

Viking that she was, Amelia was beginning to hear the call of an adventure more difficult, more dangerous, than anything she had yet undertaken. She wanted to fly the Atlantic alone, she told George. He felt pride and a whisper of fear, but he uttered no word intended to caution or restrain his wife's free spirit.

She began preparations for the flight in early spring of 1932, with Bernt Balchen, veteran airman and polar explorer, as her technical adviser.

She already owned a Lockheed Vega, capable of long-range flying. Its worn motor was replaced. Extra fuel tanks were built into the wings and another tank was installed in the cabin.

As on her first Atlantic flight, plans were kept secret. She didn't want to be distracted from the preparations by letters and telephone calls from well-wishers and the inquiries of reporters.

When the plane had been tested and was ready to go, she flew it to Teeterboro, New Jersey. On a day in late

May, when conditions over the Atlantic were judged as favorable as they would be for some time, she took off for St. John, New Brunswick. Balchen went along to handle the plane, and her mechanic went to give it a last tuneup. En route she rested in the crowded cabin, her back against the gas tank.

The trio spent the night at St. John. The next afternoon they were at Grace Harbor where the mechanic went over the plane. At sunset, lithe and boyish in her jodhpurs, silk shirt, and windbreaker, Amelia shook hands with the two men, climbed into the plane alone and flew out to sea.

For most of the voyage death flew alongside the red plane.

Her altimeter failed when night came. The instrument was made to measure altitude. Now in the dark she couldn't judge height visually.

The plane flew into a storm of high winds, rain, and lightning. The plane shuddered and fought her control.

She began to climb, trying to get above the storm. For a half hour she bore upward. It grew colder, freezing. She saw ice form and thicken on the window. Ice grew on the wings, too, impeding the flaps, but this she could not see.

Without warning, the plane went into a spin. Iced up, it could not be controlled. Through the storm and darkness it fell. Only when it was so close to the water that she could see the whitecaps did she recapture control. The descent to the warmth of near sea level had loosed the ice's hold.

She left the storm behind. Flying under the vast starlit sky she experienced beauty and peace, and a sense of comfort from the steady throb of the motor. It was a mood which danger again shattered.

Flame, like a brilliant pennant, whipped out from the

motor. A weld in the manifold ring had broken. Disaster would come if the metal burned through or the gasoline ignited.

"There was nothing I could do about it," she said later, "so it seemed sensible to keep going."

She flew through the night, an eye on the flame, hearing new danger in the rattle of the weakened metal. Day came. The fire still burned, each hour raising the odds for disaster.

She swung from her course to hunt for the nearest land, Ireland, and when the Irish coast thrust out of the sea she dropped down and headed inland, seeking an airfield. She could find none; she saw only farm land and grazing cattle. She didn't delay longer and skimmed down for a landing on a farm a half dozen miles from Londonderry.

"SHE MADE IT!" the newspapers bannered. "AMELIA FLIES THE ATLANTIC!"

King George of England expressed his pleasure to her, and Britain received her like royalty. After two weeks of being feted in London she crossed the English Channel to France, where Putnam joined her.

She was received by the French Senate, whose members paid her Gallic compliments and awarded her the Cross of Knight of the Legion of Honor.

In Italy, she and Putnam were received by the country's dictator Benito Mussolini. Mussolini showed her a condescending cordiality, for Fascism held that the kitchen was the proper place of women. To Putnam, who had published a book written by a refugee from Italian Fascism, Mussolini was cool.

Then she went to Belgium where she lunched with King Albert and his Queen who took the American's picture with an inexpensive little box camera.

On her return home Amelia was a guest of President and
Mrs. Herbert Hoover at the White House. The President
spoke at ceremonies in Washington's Constitution Hall
where Amelia was given the special gold medal of the
National Geographic Society.

"Her accomplishments," said Mr. Hoover, "combine to
place her in spirit with the great pioneering women to
whom every generation of America has looked up to with
admiration for their firmness of will, their strength of
character, and their cheerful spirit in the work of the
world. . . . Her success has not been won by the selfish
pursuit of a purely personal ambition, but as part of a career
generously animated by a wish to help others to share in
the rich opportunities of life, and by a wish also to enlarge
those opportunities by expanding the powers of women."

Soon President Franklin D. Roosevelt and Eleanor Roosevelt tenanted the White House and Amelia was several
times their guest. She and Mrs. Roosevelt became very fond
of each other.

At dinner in the White House one evening in the spring
of 1933 Amelia was telling what a joy it was to fly at night.
Mrs. Roosevelt said she had never flown after dark. "Would
you like to?" Amelia asked. "Tonight?"

Mrs. Roosevelt smiled with pleasure. "Why, yes," she
said. "Yes."

Amelia telephoned a commercial airline and asked for the
loan of a transport plane. It was granted. The two women,
in evening gowns, motored to the airport and went aloft
for a flight over Washington and Baltimore.

A news reporter wrote, "Miss Earhart piloted the big
plane without even removing her long white gloves."

In 1934 Amelia was a speaker at a conference in New
York on "Women and the Changing World" where she assailed the notion that the younger generation was drifting
and defeated.

In the audience was Dr. Edward C. Elliott, President of
Purdue University. A few weeks later he arranged to have
dinner with Amelia and her husband. Over coffee he said
to her, "We'd like you to come to Purdue."

The university, Dr. Elliott said, had an enrollment of
six thousand students, about eight hundred of them girls.
"We feel," he said, "that the girls aren't taking advantage
of the exciting opportunities of the present as well as they
might be. I think you could do much to overcome the lag."

For two hours the three of them talked about it and
Amelia, enthusiastic as always about this kind of challenge,
said, "I'd like to try it."

She was made Counselor in Careers for Women (a title
she could not bring herself to pronounce) in June of 1935.
Announcing her appointment, Dr. Elliott said:

"Miss Earhart represents better than any other young
woman of this generation the spirit and courageous skill of
what may be called the new pioneering. At no point in
our educational system is there greater need for pioneering
and constructive planning than in education for women."

She spent six weeks of the academic year at Purdue, living with the girls in one of the dormitories and taking her
meals with the students in one of the cafeterias. Very
quickly the gap caused by her age and official status was
bridged and the girls took to dropping into her room at
night to talk about matters ranging from their difficulty
with a particular course to their relations with boy friends.

One of the first things Amelia did was to conduct an analysis of the after-college plans of Purdue's girl students. More than 90 per cent planned to work. She discussed the results of the analysis with faculty members, in an effort to make the curriculum more useful.

She met with student groups in discussions of vocational opportunities and urged the girls, as far as possible, to do the things they wanted to do rather than what they thought they "should do."

Out of her own philosophy and experience she used to say, "If you want to try a certain job, then try it. Experiment. And if you find something later which you like more, make the change."

Always she urged courage and a readiness to pioneer. "If you find that you are the first woman to feel an urge to do a certain job," she used to say, "what difference does it make? If it's what you want, do it."

Amelia had a strong interest in aviation research, and in the human aspects of flying. She felt that most aviation research had concentrated on equipment and overlooked the pilot. Her interest was well known among her friends and associates.

During her second year at Purdue the university established an Amelia Earhart Fund for Aeronautical Research and purchased a large Lockheed transport plane for her, outfitting it as a flying laboratory.

She outlined a program of research into the effects of speed, altitude, changes in air pressure, fatigue, and other flying factors on those who pilot or travel in planes.

Meanwhile, she had by no means given up marathon flying. She flew from Honolulu to Oakland, California— 2,400 miles—in her flying laboratory. It was so exhausting that she dropped to the ground when she stepped out of the plane.

At the invitation of the Mexican government she flew 1,700 miles from Los Angeles to Mexico City. In the Mexican capital she managed to free herself for a time from official receptions to talk with farm women about their work, their way of life, and their hopes.

Then she flew 2,200 miles from Mexico City to Newark, New Jersey, the first time such a flight had been made nonstop. The press and radio marveled that aviation had so progressed that she could have breakfast in Mexico City (though an early one, to be sure) and supper in Newark.

In February of 1937 Amelia announced that she was going to try to fly around the world at the equator in her flying laboratory. A reporter asked her, "How long will it take?" and she answered, "I can't say. Such a flight has never been attempted. I'm simply going to fly as and when I can. I'm not going to race anyone. Eventually airplanes will find it easy to go around the world. Not only around the equator, but around every way. Every flight, therefore, is potentially important. It may yield valuable knowledge."

She added that she wanted to test the effect of various diets en route. She also wanted to determine the effect which constant studying of the numerous instruments would have on a pilot over many hours' flying.

Her route was to be west to east. She would start at Oakland, California. Honolulu would be her first stop.

A month later she set out with a crew of two and successfully flew the first leg of her trip in 15 hours and 47 minutes. In Honolulu the fliers slept; the plane was checked and loaded with gasoline.

The next morning the plane roared down the runway—

and suddenly it went out of control in what pilots call a ground loop, piling up crazily on its side. Amelia, fighting the controls, had the presence of mind to shut off the switches to prevent fire.

Neither Amelia nor the crowd of onlookers could explain what had caused the accident.

After it was determined that she was not hurt and the crewmen were also uninjured, the first question the reporters asked her was, "Will you try again?"

"Of course," she said.

On June 1 of that same year Amelia Earhart started out again. This time she reversed her route. She flew east to west, starting from Miami, Florida.

It was to be a rendezvous with death.

Dorothy Shaver

A FEW YEARS before Mary Lyon founded Mount Holyoke in 1837, Samuel Lord opened a little store on Catherine Street in New York. Later he took in his wife's cousin as a partner, and Lord and Taylor advertised in the *New York Enquirer*:

TOMORROW MORNING THE FOLLOWING
GOODS WILL BE SOLD
AT FAIR PRICES AS USUAL:

HEAVY PLAIDS FOR WINTER'S WEAR
SUPERIOR QUALITY MEN'S AND WOMEN'S SILK HOSE
BOBBINET LACE VEILS, CAPS AND COLLARS
MUSLIN BANDS, ELEGANT CASHMERE SHAWLS

In 1944 another Lord and Taylor ad appeared in the New York newspapers.

It showed a drawing of New York's Empire State Building leaning toward Paris' Eiffel Tower. The caption read:

MY, IT'S GOOD TO SEE YOU AGAIN!

That was all. No illustrations of merchandise. No announcement of a sale. No prices. Just the drawing and a few words such as any American might have exclaimed in his happiness over the great event, for Paris had just been liberated from the Germans in the Second World War.

In the century between the appearance of the two ads a revolution in merchandising philosophy had occurred. It was a revolution in which the first vice president—and soon to be president—of Lord and Taylor had taken part as a leader.

This leader in merchandising was the beneficiary of another revolution, achieved by Mary Lyon and Susan Anthony and Belva Lockwood and all the other women who fought for equality and opportunity for their sex.

Miss Dorothy Shaver was her name.

When she was elected president by the board of directors in January, 1946, the newspapers observed that for the first time in mercantile history a woman had taken over the presidency of an organization doing an annual business of as much as thirty million dollars. (The next year sales climbed to forty million.)

This was news and human interest. The reporters came to see her.

"I refused to talk about myself," she recalled. "I knew exactly what the interviewers would write. They would tell what I wore, how much makeup I used, and all the rest about a woman who has happened to make good.

"I am tired of hearing about career women. After all, women are people and should be judged as individuals, without regard to their sex. All this fuss about a woman's making good is a leftover from the time when they were not considered men's equals."

And she added: "As far as I am concerned, the fact that I happen to be a woman has not stood in my way."

Her comment was evidence of the progress women had made since Mary Lyon went from house to house pleading for funds to provide young women with a higher education.

With World War Two a receding memory, Dorothy Shaver sat in her office on the ninth floor of the Fifth Avenue store—grown into a chain of stores under her stewardship—and talked about her life and work and ideas. She loved ideas, whether formulating her own or listening to those of others. But ideas had to be big and bold. The petty ones she had no use for.

"Don't give me dibs and dabs," she would tell her staff at meetings. "Give me four big ideas a year and you can relax the rest of the time."

Her office was like a charming, period living room, her little desk at one end and a fireplace (obviously much used) at the other. There were Chippendale chairs and a breakfront, and pictures of Mr. and Mrs. Lord looked down on her. The walls were pine-paneled, smoky-hued with age.

She sat at her desk, a merchandising executive with the enthusiasm of a girl. Her dress was simple, black—what the stylists call a "basic black." It was unadorned except for a tiny tricolor at the collar: France had conferred on her the Cross of Chevalier in the Legion of Honor.

She wore no jewelry except for a bracelet, to which several heavy keys of unusual design were attached. They clinked softly as she gestured. Her luxurious hair was brown. Her handsome eyes were also brown. Except for lipstick, she wore little make-up.

Her interviewer knew that the only job she had ever had was with Lord and Taylor and he asked, "How did you happen to come to work here?"

Her eyes brightened with humor. "Lord and Taylor hired me because of a doll," she said. "Five dolls, really—the Five Little Shavers. They are characters from the fairy tales of our childhood, my sister Elsie's and mine. Our grandfather used to make them up, the most entrancing fairy stories ever told children.

"Well, Elsie made these dolls—"

She made a gesture of impatience. "It sounds confused, doesn't it?" she said. "Why don't I start at the beginning?"

She was born in Center Point, Arkansas—"a little wide place in the road," she called it—on July 29, 1897. Two or three years later her family moved to Mena, Arkansas, where father, mother, and the two boys and two girls lived in a many-roomed white Southern home with broad verandas and high columns.

Dorothy's father, James D. Shaver, was a lawyer. The townsfolk, who respected and liked the quiet-spoken man, called him Judge Shaver. In the South at that time lawyers were often called Judge as a term of respect, but Judge Shaver actually had a right to the title, for during Dorothy's early years he had served on both the federal and circuit court benches.

Mrs. Shaver, Sallie Shaver, was a serene woman, much loved and admired by her family, of great intelligence, well-read. She instilled in Dorothy (called Deedie as a child), Deedie's sister Elsie, and their brothers a feeling that life was a joy and an adventure. She also gave them a sense of responsibility to others.

Deedie's home was rich in love and happiness, and abounding in activity. There were numerous relatives and they came often for lengthy visits—parents and children. At such times the large house smelled deliciously of foods cooking and baking in the huge kitchen, and the shouts and laughter of children were heard from morning to bedtime. But most satisfying of all to Deedie was the conversation.

She loved to listen as the grown-ups, dinner over, lingered at the table for leisurely talk. So many things they knew. Such wonderful ideas they expressed.

Reading, thinking, and good conversation—these were encouraged in the Shaver children. Each child was expected, when the family dined alone, to have an item of interest to contribute to the conversation. There were times when Deedie was at a loss for a topic as the dinner hour neared. She would take a volume of the family's encyclopedia down from the shelf and read one of the entries over and over.

Judge Shaver had a good library and she knew many of its books intimately. She read Shakespeare and Dante so many times she lost count.

"The town," Miss Shaver recalled, "had a number of well-informed people who were interested in literature, music, government, and world affairs. They used to meet weekly for discussions. When they came to our home, Elsie and I always sat close by so we could listen."

At one meeting in the Shaver home the subject was books and Deedie wrote down the titles and authors of ten she heard mentioned. "They were what are termed adult books," she said.

"The town had a well-stocked library," she continued, "and I was encouraged to use it. I went there the next day with my list and asked the librarian if I could borrow the ten books. I thought she looked at me a little oddly. She excused herself and went to telephone my mother, whom she knew. She asked my mother if she knew the titles of the books I had come to borrow. My mother said calmly that it was all right."

In her home Deedie heard many anecdotes about her maternal grandfather, Major Borden, the first editor of the famous newspaper *The Arkansas Gazette*. He had fought the last legal duel in the state of Arkansas.

She had never known the Major. But she did know her other grandfather, Judge Shaver's father. He made his home with the family and was an important figure in her childhood. This was Robert—Fighting Bob—Shaver, a Confederate general in the War Between the States.

Deedie would sit with him in the garden or accompany him about the town and the old man would bring to life with his stories the great men of the Confederacy and the stirring hours of the War Between the States. Stroking his white beard, which had once been red, "Fighting Bob" would tell of college pranks he had played with his madcap roommate, James E. B. Stuart, the Jeb Stuart who later became the South's famous cavalry leader and raider. He would tell of campaigns he had fought under General Robert E. Lee and describe the religious devotion of General Stonewall Jackson.

The old man had a gift for story-telling and the long-legged, brown-eyed girl would hear the echo of cannon and shiver fearfully as General Shaver recounted how he opened the Battle of Shiloh and had three horses shot from under him. She would giggle as he told how he had captured a Union general in his nightshirt.

People, good talk, good books, ideas—these were the things the girl loved. Thus she was tremendously excited when a new rector of the Shaver family church moved into the town. He was said to have ten children and a library of ten thousand volumes.

"I had to go to their home," Miss Shaver said. "I thought how wonderful it must be to have nine brothers and sisters in the same house with you all the time. I had to see them. And all those books.

"At breakfast one day my grandfather said he was going to call on the new rector. I pleaded to go with him. His expression didn't change. He didn't say anything. When I walked with him I always held his forefinger and now, without a word, he held out his finger. It meant I was invited."

She was introduced to the rector and his wife and their children. There *were* ten. She played with the children and had pie and milk.

She asked if she could see the rector's library. She made a sample count of several shelves. "I was disappointed," Miss Shaver said. "The rumor about the books was wrong. There weren't ten thousand—only about two thousand. I spent several hours happily, playing with the children and looking at the books. But it wasn't enough. I had to listen to the conversation of my grandfather and the rector. What fascinating things could they be saying? I went to the doorway of the room where they were sitting and listened. I picked up the threads of their talk. They were discussing points of theology which they doubted or really didn't believe."

Walking home, Deedie questioned her grandfather about theology, trying to get him to talk in the same vein as he had with the rector. She was delighted with this new topic. But the old man thought these matters were too big for a little girl to discuss. Finally he said, "There's a big mystery in Oliegewob. Thomas Felix has a black eye and he's mournful. And he won't say how he got it."

In a moment he had caught Deedie's interest with his fairy story, diverting her from the subject of religion. He could always entrance her with his tales.

The stories which General Shaver told Deedie and her red-headed sister Elsie took place in a fairy land called Oliegewob. Its heroine was the Princess of Oliegewob.

"Elsie and I loved her tenderly and protectively," Miss Shaver said, "because the Princess had a great problem. In all the fairy stories we had read, princesses had tiny, pretty feet. But Princess Oliegewob had big feet, which she was always trying to hide."

Miss Shaver went on, "Oliegewob was not a Never-Never Land. As my grandfather told the stories, their events were really happening, in a world which actually was.

"Of course Elsie and I knew that the stories weren't really true. But while my grandfather was telling them they seemed to be. We got to know the little people of Oliegewob so well they took on the substance of life."

The years which spanned the interval between childhood and adolescence passed. One day she was a young lady, Deedie no longer but Miss Dorothy. Slim and graceful in white crinoline, her lustrous hair worn like a crown, she was much in demand as a dance partner at the young people's parties. The young men came calling on her at the Shaver home.

Dorothy and Elsie attended high school and Dorothy thought that after college she might try to become a magazine editor. Elsie wanted to be a painter.

Dorothy went to the University of Arkansas and then the University of Chicago, majoring in English. At the same time Elsie was a student at the Chicago Art Institute.

The sisters were happy in Chicago but New York was beckoning to them. To Elsie New York was the art center of the Western Hemisphere. There worked the painters she admired; there were the museums and galleries. Dorothy saw it as the place where one went to make his fortune, though she thought in terms of achievement rather than money. The girls talked about going there to live. Their talk wasn't really serious at first, but it was pleasant to speculate. Then they began to talk about it with some seriousness, and a little fear. And then Elsie said—or maybe it was Dorothy—"Let's go to New York." And the other sister nodded her head.

Forty-eight hours later they were in New York, thrilled and excited and wanting to see everything the first day. They rented a room and telephoned their mother, whom they had not told of their intentions. Sallie Shaver didn't get angry or flustered. She made a note of their address and said, "I'm coming to see you on the first train."

This was in the early 1920's, and years later Dorothy Shaver recalled the meeting with her mother. "She kissed us and looked us over a little anxiously," Miss Shaver said. "When she saw that we were all right she sat down and asked us why we had done such a reckless thing. She said she thought we should go back to Chicago.

"Elsie talked and I talked. We told her what New York meant to us and how strongly we wanted to stay. When it became clear to our mother that this wasn't an escapade, that we had thought it all out, she said, 'Very well, you may stay. Just take care of yourselves and write us often. But all the money you'll have is your allowance, just as at school. If you want to remain you'll have to earn money to support yourselves.'

"She was a remarkable woman, my mother," Miss Shaver said.

The girls had a little money saved and Elsie enrolled in an art school. They met an older couple who owned a house in Manhattan and the girls rented part of the house from them. The man and wife lived on the first floor, Dorothy and Elsie on the second, and on the third was a well-lighted room where Elsie could paint.

Dorothy was not sure what she wanted to do. The immediate need, she thought, was for money, money to enable Elsie to continue her art training and money to support Dorothy herself while she studied possible careers.

"We've got to make money," she impressed on Elsie and evolved idea after idea, only to discard them all as unworkable after further thinking.

But one day she had an idea for making money, and the longer she considered it, the more promising it appeared. She had remembered a magazine article about the success of the kewpie doll which an artist named Rose Latham had designed. And Elsie also was an artist.

According to the article, Rose Latham had made $50,000 from her doll.

Dorothy told her sister all that she remembered about the article and urged, "Make a doll. Something original, different. I'm sure it will go over. The kewpie proved that there's a market for something new."

Elsie liked the idea. She went to her studio room to think and sketch. She worked for days. But none of her ideas satisfied her or Dorothy. The dolls Elsie sketched seemed commonplace, and those that looked original lacked appeal.

Then out of her childhood and the fairy stories of her grandfather Elsie got an inspiration—a doll like Princess Oliegewob. She knew exactly how the doll should look for she had always seen the Princess in her mind: pretty, but not too pretty, with soft golden hair and a little look of timidity on her face that made you want to protect her. And of course with big feet.

Enthusiastically, Elsie began to sketch and as she worked her mind was working too, enriching her basic idea. Why not a companion doll for the Princess? Say, Thomas Felix. Yes, and why not a third doll from the Land of Oliegewob? Before she had finished thinking about it, Elsie had decided to make a set of five dolls. Dorothy saw immediately the worth of the idea. The sisters decided to call the dolls "The Five Little Shavers."

Elsie set to work making the dolls. Dorothy helped. Elsie used silk floss for the dolls' hair for greater realism. After making the figures, Elsie painted on their coloring and facial characteristics. Then she made and decorated an individual cardboard box for each doll. On each box she printed a little story, telling of the Land of Oliegewob, giving the name of the doll and describing its personality.

The work took weeks. For relaxation the sisters took rides on ferryboats for a nickel, went to art museums, walked about the city, and sought out interesting and in-expensive restaurants for their dinners.

A Sunday came. The couple who owned the house the sisters lived in were away for the day. Dorothy and Elsie had tea and toast for lunch and lounged about, reading the Sunday newspaper and talking. The dolls were finished.

The doorbell rang and Dorothy went to answer it. Standing at the door was a tall gentleman, gray-haired and dignified, in a shining high hat, cutaway coat, and striped trousers. A lady was by his side. The man said, "Good day. I am Mr. Reyburn and this is Mrs. Reyburn. And which Miss Shaver are you?"

"Oh, how do you do. I am Dorothy," she said. "Won't you come in, please."

After a puzzled moment she had remembered. Mrs. Shaver had written the girls that she had asked Mr. Rey-burn to look in on them. Samuel W. Reyburn also came from Arkansas and was a friend of Mrs. Shaver.

The two Shaver girls and the two older people sat in the living room. The Reyburns had been to church, and Mrs. Reyburn said she had been greatly moved by the minister's sermon; she quoted portions of it. Mr. Reyburn asked how Dorothy and Elsie liked New York and they both exclaimed, "Wonderful!" both speaking at once, and everyone laughed.

Shortly the conversation lagged and things became a lit-tle awkward. There wasn't much the Reyburns and the girls had in common. The difference in age didn't help. Everyone tried to make talk but it never went on for long and ended abruptly.

"I must do something," Dorothy told herself. Then she thought: "the dolls—at least they're something to talk about." She said hopefully to Elsie, "Perhaps Mr. and Mrs. Reyburn would like to see our dolls? Why don't you bring them down."

Elsie gave her sister a look which said that she didn't have much hope, but she went upstairs and came down with the dolls in their boxes. The girls showed the dolls and read the legends on the boxes. They told the Reyburns about General Shaver's fairy stories. They hoped to market the dolls, they said.

Mrs. Reyburn was charmed with the "Five Little Shavers." "They're delightful," she said. "Do you think I could purchase a set when you market them?" Mr. Reyburn examined each doll carefully. He asked many questions. He wanted to know how long it would take the girls to make duplicate sets, now that they had created the originals. He asked how much they expected to be paid.

When the Reyburns had left, Dorothy and Elsie remarked that Mr. Reyburn had showed a lot of interest in the dolls. "What does he do?" Elsie asked. Dorothy said she didn't know. Mrs. Shaver had not mentioned that in her letter. The next day the girls found out.

Four men called on them. They introduced themselves by name and one said, "We're from Lord and Taylor," adding, "Mr. Reyburn told us about your dolls. Would you mind showing them to us?"

The girls looked puzzled. Dorothy said, "Mr. Reyburn—?" She made a bewildered gesture, wondering what connection there was between Mr. Reyburn and these men. One of the men saw that she didn't understand. "Mr. Reyburn—the president," he said. "You know, the president of Lord and Taylor."

One of the men was the toy manager of the department

store. Another was the advertising manager. The men examined the dolls and their hand-decorated boxes and Dorothy told them about the fairy stories of Oliegewob.

The toy manager said that Lord and Taylor would buy a supply of the dolls. He advised the girls to begin turning them out in quantity. Dorothy and Elsie were happy to say they would.

In the meantime, said the advertising manager, Lord and Taylor would like to display the dolls. Could he borrow them? The girls said yes.

All of the Fifth Avenue store's show windows were given over to a display of the dolls. They remained for two weeks, during which thousands of people stopped to look at them and many went into the store to place orders.

Meanwhile the firm of Dorothy and Elsie Shaver went into production. They rented an empty loft and hired workers, teaching them specialized tasks for greater efficiency. Some made heads, some clothing and some painted the faces.

The first shipment of dolls went to Lord and Taylor. Then Dorothy and Elsie went to other department and toy stores, selling their dolls. The business grew, providing the sisters with the financial security they had sought.

The doll business often brought Dorothy to Lord and Taylor for talks with various department heads. She didn't know this at the time, but while she was talking business she was being evaluated for something Lord and Taylor thought might be even more rewarding for them both than the "Five Little Shavers."

In time the management summed up the results of its evaluation. It concluded that the charming young woman with so much enthusiasm and so many ideas was executive material. Lord and Taylor offered her a job as head of its comparison-shopping bureau.

She had never considered a career in retailing. But she thought it over and decided she would like it. She accepted.

Dorothy Shaver had found her place, a place receptive to ideas and friendly to her talents. From now on her personal growth would be swift.

The year was 1924 when she went to work in what henceforth she would call "the store." It was an important job which had been entrusted to the untrained and unexperienced young woman. But, compared with what followed, it was nothing: three years later she was elected to the board of directors of Lord and Taylor. Her ideas, more than anything else, were the prime cause of her rise.

Although the names they give them may differ, virtually all large stores maintain comparison-shopper units. Essentially, they carry on merchandising espionage. Doing their best to look like customers, comparison-shoppers go into competing stores to ascertain the prices of various items so that the shopper's store can maintain its prices on a competitive level.

As she acquired experience and knowledge in her work, Dorothy Shaver began to feel a dissatisfaction with the philosophy of comparison-shopping. She fretted over the furtiveness of the comparison-shopper's role.

Comparison-shopping, she saw, was at best a defensive maneuver or a catching-up technique. It was incapable of giving a store a solid achievement, a real gain in the competitive realm of merchandising.

Then what could? This was the question her mind grappled with next. What strategy, what means, could provide "the store" with a positive advantage?

She devised an answer. It was so simple it is surprising no one had thought of it before. And so effective that it gave Lord and Taylor the leadership in a significant new trend in retailing.

She thought of a new type of unit, or bureau, in the store. Its function would be to improve merchandise, to work with manufacturers and strive to develop products which were unique and superior in design and quality. These products would be sold exclusively at Lord and Taylor. Telling her superiors about her plan, she said, "Then there can be no price competition. No store can take our customers away by selling the same item a few cents cheaper. Other stores just wouldn't have the item."

They liked her idea at Lord and Taylor and she was encouraged to think it through in detail and put it in writing. Years later Miss Shaver told of the evening she put on paper a description of her new bureau of stylists and its pattern of organization.

"After I left work," she said, "I went to a little coffee shop near the store, taking a good supply of paper and pencils with me. I had a pack of cigarettes in my purse and I ordered a small pot of coffee.

"Many Southerners like to carry coins, even silver dollars, instead of paper money. I spread my coins on the table and on a sheet of paper, near the top, I drew a circle around a silver dollar. That represented the position of the head of the new bureau. With my pencil I circled two half dollars for the assistants' positions, and used quarters, nickels, pennies and dimes for the other personnel. On another piece of paper I described how the bureau would function and set forth its goals."

The store management approved her plans and appointed her to direct the bureau of stylists while continuing her supervision of the comparison-shopping unit.

"I wanted to give up my comparison-shopping duties so I could concentrate exclusively on the new operation," Miss Shaver said. "I told the management that I wasn't needed in comparison-shopping. I said that my assistant could do the job as well as I. But the management was smarter than I was. They wanted to slow me down, to compel me to make the shift in emphasis a gradual one. And this was just what happened when I had to direct both the old and the new operations."

Personnel, interviewed by Dorothy Shaver, were hired for the new bureau. They were specialists in various types of merchandise. They consulted with manufacturers and advised them, in an endeavor to develop merchandise unique in quality and design.

Dorothy Shaver went to Europe to learn what designers and manufacturers there were doing and to buy for the store. It was the first of many trips abroad.

Years later she called a visitor's attention to the mellowed pine paneling on the walls of her office and said, "That taught me one of the most important lessons I ever learned in business—to use your judgment."

She had gone to England on one of her early trips, looking for antiques to buy for the store. "In an old English home," she said, "I found this paneling. Its great age was fully authenticated. I knew immediately it was a treasure.

"I also knew its dimensions were perfect for the president's office, here at the store. But instead of buying it I made the error of cabling the general manager for permission. He cabled back, NO.

"I was greatly upset. I knew I was right and the general manager was wrong. I thought it over and bought the paneling, against orders. When I got home I had some explaining to do but my reasoning was accepted.

"I told the general manager that I should never have asked him in the first place. He hadn't seen the paneling, so he couldn't possibly make a proper decision about it.

"I had been sent to buy—so I bought."

She was learning a good deal about merchandising in her years as head of the bureau of stylists, and about administration and advertising and personnel affairs. At the same time, she was developing her gift for leadership. This was based on a respect and liking for people and an understanding of their need to find satisfaction in their work. When she became president of the store she often would station herself at one of the doors at quitting time so she could see the faces of the employees as they went home.

"People don't work only for money," Miss Shaver said. "That's important, but they also want to express themselves, to be accepted and recognized. I can see by the looks on their faces when they have obtained these satisfactions. They have helped a customer solve a shopping problem. They have contributed an idea to the operation of the store or had a part in something interesting or useful."

When she was still young in experience at the store she already had thought through this concept and was applying it. The people in her bureau of stylists worked in an atmosphere conducive to bold thinking and creativity. They knew their ideas would always get a sympathetic hearing and that they would not be criticized when their ideas were faulty.

Miss Shaver believed that most people do not use their full potential, and she would try to stimulate her staff to draw deeply on its resources. "Stretch," she would urge at meetings, spreading wide her arms. "Stretch. Play the whole piano, not just a few keys."

Under her leadership the bureau of stylists acquired merchandise which was exclusively Lord and Taylor's, and therefore immune to price-cutting competition. The most significant contributions were hers. One of these revolutionized the American fashion industry.

Dorothy Shaver went often to Paris to consult with leading French designers of women's clothes and purchase their creations for the store, for Paris at that time was without a rival as the style center of the world.

Today there are many famous designers in America. There were none in the mid-twenties. There were designers, yes. But they worked in the back rooms of dress manufacturers. They were poorly paid. Their designs were used mostly for inexpensive garments.

Returning from a visit to Paris, Dorothy Shaver reasoned: "Surely America has talent equal to that of France. But our people have never been given recognition or encouragement. Their creations have never been given a value."

Home again, she began working on a plan to establish American designers on a par with those of Paris. She visited dress manufacturers on New York's Seventh Avenue and talked with the managements and their designers. She appealed to the manufacturers to produce the work of their designers in better-quality fabrics and with finer details. She appealed to the designers to surpass anything they had done before. Lord and Taylor, she said, intended to feature the creations of American designers and would purchase the most pleasing and interesting ones.

Dorothy Shaver set out to create a market for American fashion creations, striving to enhance the status and desirability of American designs. They were set off in window displays and advertised in the newspapers. The store also began to popularize the names of American designers.

Dorothy Shaver gave the name, "The American Look," to the new group of creations. Defining the "look," one series of advertisements said: "It's looking gay and fresh rather than worldly and too wise." Later there were many "looks" in incoming fashions but Dorothy Shaver used the term for the first time.

After Lord and Taylor began to promote American stylists, a woman designer whose name is now known to virtually every style-conscious woman in the forty-nine states —but who was obscure then—called Dorothy Shaver on the telephone.

"I want to thank you for what you are doing," the designer said. "Today was the first time that my boss said good morning to me since I came to work here."

As the American Look began to sell, and women who were the pacemakers in style began to adopt it, it was inevitable that other stores all over the country would begin to carry the new fashion and encourage the trend with their own promotions.

And the American fashion industry was lifted to a new level of prestige and reward.

Dorothy Shaver herself put eight years into the development of her idea, publicizing and promoting the work of more than sixty young designers. Such designers as Adrian, Claire McCardell, Clare Potter, Merry Hull, Nettie Rosenstein, and Lilly Daché got their first recognition and encouragement from her.

Dorothy Shaver's interest in women's clothes derived only partly from their value as merchandise. Dorothy shared her sister Elsie's love of art and she looked on women's clothes as another art form. To her the styling and design of these garments was a creative activity.

In promoting the work of American designers she got a great deal of gratification from an awareness that she was helping creative people.

Her interest later led her into another undertaking, intended to further the recognition of clothing style and design as an art form. After she was made president of Lord and Taylor she was instrumental in establishing a Costume Institute in New York's Metropolitan Museum of Art. There costumes of many periods and places are on display and are viewed by the public, art students, and, frequently, by designers—for the costumes of earlier periods often are the inspiration for the styles of today.

Miss Shaver became the president and chairman of the advisory committee for the Institute and a member of the Board of Trustees of the Metropolitan Museum.

In 1927 she was elected to the board of directors of Lord and Taylor. Four years later she was elected a vice-president; and in 1937 she was named first vice-president, with responsibility for style and fashion origination and promotion, and the advertising, public relations, and display programs.

She became a notable figure in New York, a tall, handsome woman with warm brown eyes and rich brown hair which she takes care of herself. At business she usually wears a dressmaker suit in navy blue or black, and plain opera pumps. She wears no hat and carries the most delicate and sheer white linen handkerchiefs. At home she likes to change into lounging clothes, usually gay and colorful.

She and Elsie acquired a house near the East River where Elsie's paintings of children and lovely ladies were hung in the high-ceilinged living room, a room decorated in pink and old white and furnished with pieces Dorothy had purchased in France.

A good citizen, she interested herself in movements dedicated to public health, education, welfare, youth, and the betterment of international relations. Over the years she became a member of the board of directors of the Menninger Foundation for research and training in psychiatry, the sponsoring committee of the American Association for the United Nations, the board of directors of the Federation of Protestant Welfare Agencies, and the Woman's Council of the New York Public Library. She also served as chairman of the board of the Girls Clubs of America.

She felt no need for hobbies. "I find my relaxation at the store," she used to say. She and Elsie bought a country home in upstate New York and went there for occasional weekends and vacations. But the vacations she liked best were spent in travel, visiting foreign lands.

In 1930 she sailed for Europe, telling Elsie she wanted to visit Sweden. When Elsie next heard from her sister, Dorothy was in Russia, a country few Americans had seen since the Communist revolution. "I wanted to see what was going on there," Dorothy explained.

When she took over responsibility for Lord and Taylor's advertising, publicity, and display, Dorothy Shaver adopted two themes as the basis of her program. The first was an outgrowth of her earlier idea for developing unique merchandise: the store's advertising and display would also be unique, she decided. They would be distinctive, instantly associated in the public's mind with Lord and Taylor. The second theme called for emphasizing the social and civic role of the store.

Under her leadership, the store's advertising illustrations became so interesting and attractive that they acquired a following. Fans, actually.

Lord and Taylor advertisements in the newspapers stopped mentioning prices, sizes, or colors; they just showed a model in a new gown or coat or a new style of shoes. Advertising experts shook their heads doubtfully, but the ads "pulled."

She demonstrated that advertisements which drew a chuckle could also sell merchandise. On one occasion she called the head of her art department to her office and instructed him, "Please draw me the biggest, blackest elephant you can."

The subsequent ad showed the elephant on a full newspaper page. Small print said:

> Everyone has a sense of smell
> Perfumes at Lord and Taylor

How the fact that even an elephant can smell influenced people to buy perfumes at Lord and Taylor remains a mystery, but the store sold thousands of dollars' worth.

Another famous Lord and Taylor ad showed a giraffe with an extra-long neck. The entire neck was draped with neckties.

She even ordered advertisements which showed just a gown or a fur coat or frilly pajamas, but made no mention of the store. When she did this for the first time her own staff thought she had gone out of her mind. She told them confidently, "Just be prepared."

Thousands of people came to buy—they recognized the store by the individuality of the ad.

Often Lord and Taylor ads advertised nothing, but used the space to recognize a civic cause or a national or religious holiday.

When Dorothy Shaver was still new in her post as first vice-president she drew international attention to Lord and Taylor with a window display.

In the early winter of 1938 America was still in an economic depression. Merchants looked with hope to the Christmas-shopping season to make up for the subnormal business of the previous months of the year.

Immediately after Thanksgiving, department stores usually install Christmas merchandise in their windows: toys, clothing, jewelry—all kinds of tempting items which people might give as gifts.

Lord and Taylor's display crew pulled out the pre-Thanksgiving merchandise from the bank of Fifth Avenue windows—and not one item of merchandise was put in the new displays. These consisted of golden bells against a white and black velvet background. In every window the bells tolled out their chimes.

Displays of this kind are not uncommon now. But they were a sensation in 1938. The bells stayed in the windows for six weeks while day-and-night crowds clogged the sidewalks before Lord and Taylor, and motorists slowed their cars to look.

Newspapers throughout America and in a number of foreign countries told their readers about the Christmas bells in Lord and Taylor's windows. Stores from as far off as China wrote Lord and Taylor for photographs of the exhibit so that they could duplicate it.

Twenty-two years after joining Lord and Taylor, Dorothy Shaver was elected president of the store.

Member newspapers of the Associated Press voted her the outstanding woman in business.

The American Schools and Colleges Association gave her its Horatio Alger Award.

Meanwhile, Dorothy Shaver was leading the Lord and Taylor organization to further achievement and growth. Under her direction Lord and Taylor became the first store in America to establish a junior department, a department for teen-age clothing, and a shop for women five-feet-four and under, the 54 Shop. Lord and Taylor also set precedents by establishing a budget shop, a college shop, a bride shop, and a maternity shop.

Each of these was widely imitated.

Appreciating the significance of the movement of population to the suburbs, she opened a suburban store, in Manhasset, New York. The new store was designed for maximum shopping ease in artistic surroundings. Subsequently Lord and Taylor added six more suburban stores, in Millburn, New Jersey; Westchester, New York; West Hartford, Connecticut; Garden City, New York; Bala-Cynwyd, near Philadelphia; and Washington, D.C.

While growing economically, Lord and Taylor also was playing a civic role. Almost from her beginning with Lord and Taylor, Dorothy Shaver believed that this was a duty of a large department store.

In 1928, with material she had collected abroad, she organized in the store an exhibition titled *"L'Art Décoratif et la Peinture Française."* It was perhaps the first comprehensive exhibit in America of modern decorative art and gave great impetus to the development of modern decorative art in the United States.

For opening night the store was filled with red roses, and guests in formal dress supped on salads and champagne and admired fabrics, rugs, paintings, and silver in nine exhibition rooms.

Ten years later Dorothy Shaver organized the annual Lord and Taylor American Design Awards. The first ones recognized two clothes designers, Clare Potter and Nettie Rosenstein, and two textile designers, Dorothy Liebes and Stanislav V'Soske.

The first time the awards were given the event received little attention. Announcements were sent to the newspapers and radio stations and the designers came to Miss Shaver's office to pick up their awards of one thousand dollars each.

Soon Miss Shaver gave the program a much broader scope. The Lord and Taylor Awards, as they came to be called, were given in recognition of achievement in all spheres of endeavor which benefited humanity.

By 1945 some eighteen hundred guests were attending the Awards luncheon at the Waldorf-Astoria when a grant of $25,000 was given the National Academy of Science.

Since then Awards have been given to, among others, the Sloan-Kettering Institute for Cancer Research, to Albert Einstein, to Dr. Ralph Bunche, American Negro diplomat, to an adult counseling center, to the United Nations Food and Agriculture Organization, and to Dr. Leona Baum-gartner, Director of the Bureau of Child Hygiene of New York City.

With these awards, Dorothy Shaver pioneered in corporate public service. A preface to the announcement of the 1958 Awards said that they were, "Presented in the belief in the power of creative thought as the central catalyst for human progress."

An anecdote is told in Lord and Taylor's about Dorothy Shaver:

She went to the office of one of her executives to discuss plans for a new store. A secretary took notes while Miss Shaver and the executive talked.

When Dorothy Shaver had left, the secretary shook her head admiringly. "What a woman!" she said.

To which the man replied, "Thought has no sex."

Bibliography

MARY LYON

Oliver Jensen, *The Revolt of American Women*. Harcourt, Brace & Company, New York, 1952.

Marian F. Lansing, *Mary Lyon Through Her Letters*. Books, Inc., New York, 1937.

Willystine Goodsell, *The Education of Women*. The Macmillan Company, New York, 1923.

Arthur C. Cole, *A Hundred Years of Mount Holyoke College*. Yale University Press, New Haven, 1940.

Beth Bradford Gilchrist, *The Life of Mary Lyon*. Houghton Mifflin Company, Boston, 1910.

Robert E. Riegel, *Young America*. University of Oklahoma Press, Norman, Okla., 1949.

SUSAN B. ANTHONY

Sherwood Eddy and Kirby Page, *Makers of Freedom*. George H. Doran Company, New York, 1926.

Don C. Seitz, *Uncommon Americans*. Bobbs-Merrill Company, Inc., Indianapolis, 1925.

M. A. DeWolfe Howe, *Causes and Their Champions*. Little, Brown and Company, Boston, 1926.

Rheta Child Dorr, *Susan B. Anthony*. Frederick A. Stokes Company, New York, 1928.

Ida Husted Harper, *The Life and Work of Susan B. Anthony*. Bowen-Merrill Company, Indianapolis, 1898.

Katherine Anthony, *Susan B. Anthony*. Doubleday & Company, Garden City, N.Y., 1954.

Constance Burnett, *Five for Freedom*. Abelard Press, Inc., New York, 1953.

BELVA ANN LOCKWOOD

National Magazine, March, 1903.

Literary Digest, June 16, 1917.

Inez H. Irwin, *Angels and Amazons*. Doubleday, Doran & Company, New York, 1933.

Material in the Women's Archives of Radcliffe College, Cambridge, Mass.

Laura Kerr, *The Girl Who Ran for President*. Thomas Nelson & Sons, New York, 1947.

ANTOINETTE BROWN

Unpublished letters and papers in the possession of Horace B. Robinson, New York (Antoinette Brown's grandson).

Laura Kerr, *Lady in the Pulpit*. Womans Press, New York, 1951.

Frances Hosford, *Father Shipherd's Magna Charta*. Marshall Jones Company, Boston, 1937.

Robert S. Fletcher, A *History of Oberlin College*. Oberlin College Press, Oberlin, Ohio, 1943.

The Bulletin of Oberlin College, New Series 343.

ALICE HAMILTON

Alice Hamilton, *Exploring the Dangerous Trades*. Little, Brown and Company, Boston, 1943.

Edna Yost, *American Women of Science*. J. B. Lippincott Company, Philadelphia, 1955.

LILLIAN M. GILBRETH

Frank B. Gilbreth, *Primer of Scientific Management*. D. Van Nostrand Co., Inc., Princeton, N.J., 1912.

Edna Yost, *Partners for Life*. Rutgers University Press, New Brunswick, N.J., 1949.

Frank B. Gilbreth, Jr., and Ernestine Gilbreth Carey, *Cheaper by the Dozen*. Thomas Y. Crowell Company, New York, 1949.

Frank B. Gilbreth, Jr., and Ernestine Gilbreth Carey, *Belles on Their Toes*. Thomas Y. Crowell Company, New York, 1950.

The Journal of the California Teachers Association, April, 1956.

The American Girl, September, 1943.

Lillian M. Gilbreth, *Living with Our Children*. W. W. Norton & Co., Inc., New York, 1951.

AMELIA EARHART

Amelia Earhart, *The Fun of It*. Junior Literary Guild, New York, 1932.

Amelia Earhart, *20 Hrs. 40 Min.* G. P. Putnam's Sons, New York, 1928.

Amelia Earhart, *Last Flight*. Harcourt, Brace & Company, New York, 1937.

George Palmer Putnam, *Soaring Wings*. Harcourt, Brace & Company, New York, 1939.

Betty Peckham, *Women in Aeronautics*. Thomas Nelson & Sons, New York, 1945.

DOROTHY SHAVER

New York Times Magazine, January 5, 1947.

Good Housekeeping Magazine, October, 1956.

Vogue Magazine, February 1, 1946.

Book of Knowledge Supplement, 1949.

Life Magazine, May 12, 1947.

House and Garden Magazine, January, 1947.

INDEX

ABOUT THE AUTHOR

David K. Boynick was born in Boston and attended public school there. As a boy he sold newspapers on historic Boston Common, and his many hours in the wintery winds paid off when he later was the recipient of the Newsboys Foundation and Harvard College Scholarship.

Mr. Boynick was a newspaperman for fifteen years before he became the Assistant Commissioner of Mental Health of Connecticut. He now lives in Hartford with his wife and two children, and his work is concerned with research and with breaking down public prejudice and fear of mental illness.

Pioneers in Petticoats is Mr. Boynick's second book, and when asked what led him to write it he said, "I think I was prompted by the same feeling that led to my writing *Champions by Setback*. I have a strong sympathy for people who have been handicapped. Women have historically been handicapped."

Date Due

APR 8 '60			
JUL 11 '62			
DEC 10 '62			
JAN 16 '63			
SEP 29 '65			
OCT 13 '65			
9			
MR 10 '69			
MY 19 '73			
AP 8 '74			
SE 25 '74			
DE 9 '74			
DE 21 '74			
FE 14 '83			
JE 16 '83			
NO 5 '84			
JA 25 '88			
FE 15 '89			
MY 2 '90			